WAKING FROM DOCTRINAL AMNESIA

Waking from Doctrinal Amnesia

The Healing of Doctrine in The United Methodist Church

WILLIAM J. ABRAHAM

ABINGDON PRESS / Nashville

WAKING FROM DOCTRINAL AMNESIA:
THE HEALING OF DOCTRINE IN THE UNITED METHODIST CHURCH

Copyright © 1995 by Abingdon Press

This book is printed on acid-free, recycled paper.

Library of Congress Cataloging-in-Publication Data

Abraham, William J. (William James), 1947–
    Waking from doctrinal amnesia: the healing of doctrine in the
United Methodist Church/William J. Abraham.
        p.   cm.
    Includes bibliographical references and index.
    ISBN 0-687-01718-1 (pbk.: alk. paper)
    1. United Methodist Church (U.S.)—Doctrines.   2. United Methodist
Church (U.S.)—Membership.   3. Methodist Church—United States—
Doctrines.   4. Methodist Church—United States—Membership.
5. United States—Church history—20th century.   I. Title.
BX8331.2.A27 1995
230'.76'09045—dc20   95-37009
                                                                        CIP

95 96 97 98 99 00 01 02 03 04—10 9 8 7 6 5 4 3 2 1

MANUFACTURED IN THE UNITED STATES OF AMERICA

To Bob Irish

Contents

Acknowledgments

The argument outlined here has been germinating in my mind for almost ten years. It would be impossible to record the debts I owe to a host of people who have contributed to my reflection. I want in particular to thank Scott Jones, Elizabeth Moreau, Keefe Cropper, John Feagins, and Dianne Knippers for sharing their ideas with me. A very special word of thanks goes to my research assistant, Julie Halstead, whose ready wit, editorial eye, and good judgment have been invaluable at various stages of the process.

I am extremely grateful to my colleagues in the Southwest Texas Annual Conference and to my bishop, Ray Owen, for inviting me to share some of this material with them in the spring of 1994. A preliminary and very brief version of the argument in the last three chapters was developed in "The Revitalization of United Methodist Doctrine and the Renewal of Evangelism," in James C. Logan, ed., *Theology and Evangelism in the Wesleyan Heritage* (Nashville: Kingswood Books, 1994). I am also extremely grateful to Jill Reddig for her wonderful support and her astute advice.

On a wider front, this work is part of a much longer project on authority and divine agency which I am currently undertaking as a scholar with the Pew Evangelical Scholars Initiative. When I began that work I did not realize the significance of that project for the understanding of the doctrinal situation within United Methodism. So this material represents a delightful surprise on a long and arduous journey made possible

9

by the Pew Charitable Trust. I am grateful beyond words for this utterly invaluable help.

Finally, I want to thank my wife, Muriel, who knows more than anyone all that I owe to her.

Chapter One

Unity and Disunity in The United Methodist Church

AN APPEAL FOR REASONED ARGUMENT

How are we to describe the current state of The United Methodist Church? Has it become, as John Wesley feared it might become, a dead sect holding the form but denying the power of true religion? Is it quietly sliding into oblivion, sharing the fate of all mainline Protestantism, as it continues to lose numbers and status in society? Or is it in the process of reinventing itself by relating, say, in its heavy use of church growth strategies, to the values of a changed culture? Is it taking stock in order to muster its vast energy and resources for a fresh wave of service, as it marches into a new millennium? Or is it going through a radical new reformation, prophetically leading the modern American church into the kind of fundamental revision that will be needed for mission in a new day? Is it providing the kind of theological leadership it provided in the late nineteenth century when it championed the merits of Liberal Protestantism? Or is it on the brink of explicit apostasy? Has it, with its enthusiasm for pluralism, paved the way for a radical reworking of the Christian faith which will undermine it from within?

However we frame our questions, there is no doubt that many United Methodist leaders are currently engaged in a very serious soul-searching concerning the future of the church. Some fear that we are so internally divided that we are really facing the prospects of schism. Others see in the

11

very mention of schism an attempt to use fear tactics in order to tilt the tradition in a radically conservative direction. They are convinced that United Methodism is inherently a pluralist denomination, so that any attempt to take the church down a conservative road is a serious defection from the faith on a par with the Fundamentalist takeover of the Southern Baptist tradition. Yet others would prefer to leave things as they are on the grounds that self-analysis is really a form of self-indulgence; we cannot afford, they say, to allow ourselves to be distracted from the real challenges that lie before us in the immediate future. Still others remain quiet, because they are fearful that analysis might expose fissures which cannot really be sealed; better to muddle through, they think, than run the risk of making visible the deep incoherence of the tradition as a whole.

There is, of course, a time to talk and a time to be silent. It is now time to talk. One reason for this is that traditions are like extended conversations across the generations. Healthy conversation is absolutely essential to their well-being. Of course, should the conversation become a monologue or should it descend into a brawl, then the conversation will harm the tradition. However, without conversation the tradition will not be internalized. Its problems will not be worked through, and its members will tend to take too much of the status quo for granted. In the end, if there is no conversation, the tradition will die.

In this introductory chapter I provide some background orientation for the conversation and argument which follows. The book as a whole is an attempt to come to terms with some crucial issues currently being discussed within United Methodism. My central claim is that United Methodists have been suffering from a kind of doctrinal amnesia. They have systematically forgotten the place of Christian doctrine in their life and service to God. As a result they have not been able to appreciate the predicament thrown up by their own internal squabbles. Nowhere is this more visible than in the debate about the worship of Sophia and the events surrounding the Reimagining Conference in Minneapolis.[1] Yet it would be a serious mistake to focus on this matter alone. The debate about Reimagining is the tip of a massive iceberg.

Inherent in the argument which follows is the claim that matters of Christian doctrine are inescapable. To put it simply, United Methodists are deeply confused about their doctrinal identity. This accounts not just for a whole series of problems that they face; it also accounts for the distrust and anger which all too readily surfaces when United Methodists attempt to talk to one another. In short, there really is a kind of internal schism in the church, but the fear that facing this will mean the opening of a Pandora's box prevents many United Methodist leaders from coming to terms with the question of doctrinal identity and from engaging in the kind of honest conversation which is essential. When they come within earshot of the conversation, their natural tendency is to insist that the crucial issue is not one of doctrine but one of therapy. They believe that the solution to the present ills is reconciliation or inner healing. They think that the really deep issue is a lack of love, of sympathy, of tolerance, of spiritual integrity, of affection, and the like. They have enormous difficulty grappling with the possibility that the relevant considerations are intellectual and doctrinal. They cannot face the fact that most of those involved in the current disputes are people of rocklike integrity who disagree on first principles, which are irreparably doctrinal in character. More positively, they ignore the crucial place that doctrine has in the healing of the church.

What is a church to do when it is faced with incompatible and competing doctrinal proposals in its midst? How are we to address disputes about what constitutes the proper way to identify the doctrines of a tradition? Can such identity disputes be resolved in a rational and persuasive manner?

13

Even if we want to approach the matter rationally, is there in fact adequate evidence to call on to discuss and evaluate? If there is not, then we really are at the mercy of this or that faction in the church. Whether a particular group is in or out of power is entirely secondary. The outcome in either case will be the outcome of an unseemly power struggle. This is precisely what many distinguished scholars now believe. If they are right, we are in for difficult days ahead. Yet I dare to believe otherwise.

One reason for rejecting the claim that all we are up against is a display of power is that it represents an immediate departure from the whole ethos of United Methodism. From the beginning Methodists were intentionally committed to Christian conference and reasoned argument. John Wesley was determined to make his appeal to reason, despite the fact that his opponents were determined to make the issue one of passion or emotion. The burden of my argument in the third and fourth chapters is that to reject the way of conversation and reason is not only a counsel of despair, it is a serious mistake. United Methodist doctrine can actually be identified. It is not an amorphous body of vague proposals. Nor is it some malleable theological method which can be twisted to fit this or that fad or convention of the culture. United Methodist doctrine is substantial; it is identifiable; and it is clear in its fundamental content. Until we face this, some of the central issues confronting the church will remain unresolved. Most especially, we will not even be able to begin to get an angle on whether a conference sponsored by the church or in which the church participates is or is not in keeping with the tradition.

I am well aware of the radical and revisionary nature of my suggestions. In the course of my argument I call into question the common way of understanding what it is to be United Methodist, as that has been assumed and taught over the last thirty years. I am also aware, as will be plain from

14

my fifth and last chapter, that there are significant consequences, given my analysis, for the ordering of the life of the church, which need to be explored with care. However, the time is long gone when United Methodists can rest satisfied with the consensus on doctrine which has held sway in the church for at least a generation. If nothing else, the current deep divisions ought to awaken the church from its dogmatic sleepwalking and force it to come to terms with the deep inadequacy of its current position.

The only way to deal with divisions and factions is to think systematically and critically about the very identity of the tradition. In the end this is the way in which the church down through the ages has always had to deal with internal division and disagreement. There is no way any longer to appeal to the state to enforce some kind of solution. Even when this has happened in the past, as happened in many of the Reformation churches, the relevant intellectual work had to be done to carry the day, as the brilliant work of Richard Hooker in the Anglican tradition makes clear. Contrary to what many believe, such systematic and critical reflection on doctrinal identity is not a matter of mere personal opinion; nor is it a matter of who can muster the most power or money. There are substantial reasons and considerations which have to be faced and worked through. Decisions about the issues in hand must be made on the basis of evidence and argument. To be sure the evidence is not always obvious, nor are the arguments lacking in subtlety. However, that there is relevant evidence and that cogent arguments can be mounted is beyond dispute. Indeed in the case of The United Methodist Church there is very hard evidence available. In this case, then, all factions and groups have to let the chips fall where they will. To change the metaphor, everybody has to face the music. Not just any old or new song can legitimately be described as United Methodist in content.

My own attempts to face the music have preoccupied me almost from my arrival in the United States ten years ago

15

after serving in the Irish Methodist Church. There is a special affinity, I suspect, between Irish and American Methodists. In actual fact it was Irish lay people who first brought Methodism to America. Whether we choose Barbara Heck and Philip Embury or we choose Robert Strawbridge as the first Methodists in America, either way the first Methodists were from Ireland. I came to faith within Irish Methodism and owe to the Methodist people on both sides of the Atlantic more than could ever be recorded on paper. On coming to serve God in United Methodism at a local and regional level, I have again and again been forced to think deeply about the transition and translation of the Methodist tradition from the Old to the New World. I have also pondered again and again what happened to the Methodist experiment, as it adjusted in its own unique way to the pressures of American culture and to the inner logic of its own life on a new continent. Attempting to internalize and own the tradition has been a salutary intellectual and spiritual experience.

Partly through accident and partly through design I have come into contact with representative cross-sections of the church. As a scholar I have been invited to lecture in numerous settings across the country. As a guest preacher I have spent untold hours in a host of local churches. I have been involved in the various conferences of the church in different ways. Wherever I have gone, the first order of business for me has been to get my bearings. Frankly, one never knows what one will meet as regards what United Methodists believe and hold dear. At times I have felt that I have been negotiating minefields where putting a single foot wrong would ruin any prospect of ministry or even the possibility of genuine conversation. Should one be identified with the wrong party or the wrong cause, then the game was over; one might as well pack one's bags and go home to one's books and classes. Right through the church as a whole one senses fault lines of division and disagreement which run to the very core of the tradition. One watches walls of mutual incomprehension go up which could easily lead one to quiet cynicism and despair.

THE CASE OF THE CONFUSING CONFERENCE

Nowhere has this become more visible than in the controversy surrounding the Reimagining Conference in Minneapolis. It will take years to sort out what exactly happened at that conference and to identify its significance for the future of the church and the ecumenical movement. Yet listening carefully to the debate I detect two competing readings which might well serve to illustrate the depth of division concerning identity that we face. This is not to say that these are the only readings available; indeed it would be ludicrous to think that there are two and only two readings of this event. Controversial and complex conferences are subject to a host of rival interpretations. In this case, however, it is useful to focus for a moment on two standard interpretations which are very conspicuously in the air. For the purposes of this discussion we shall refer to the rival accounts as respectively that of the defenders and that of the critics.

THE ARGUMENT OF THE DEFENDERS

The argument of the defenders runs something like this. The Reimagining Conference was a landmark occasion in which the Christian church was engaged in an updating and revision of the faith in order to make it more true to the gospel and more viable for modern women. Given this, the use of Sophia as a name for God is nothing startling; it represents an appeal to a biblical term which helps capture the feminine dimension of the divine. Indeed the whole effort to reimagine the faith by creatively finding alternative ways to think and speak about God, the person and work of Christ, salvation, the church, sexual morality, family life,

17

service in the world, and the like, is simply an attempt to allow women to find their voice and make their contribution to the life of the church in their own way.

Permitting women such a voice will cleanse the church of patriarchy and enable it to find a more just embodiment in its structural life. That alternative liturgies which focused on women's experience were used in these circumstances is entirely natural. It was equally natural that Christians from other cultures should draw on material from other religious traditions, for these other religious traditions represent a rich deposit of experience which has a right to be deployed in indigenous expressions of the Christian faith. Moreover, appeal to women's experience across a wide spectrum of cultural, class, age, and sexual orientation, constitutes an entirely proper base for Christian theology. After all, experience has been the bedrock of expositions for conceptions of the faith throughout the modern period.

The same point can be made in terms of the activity of the Holy Spirit. From time to time the Holy Spirit leads the people of God into new truth. At the time of this new revelation this truth may have appeared strange to traditionalists, but this kind of negative reaction is to be expected. Across the generations, Christians have expressed the gospel in the categories of their culture, and each successive shift of meaning has always threatened those committed to the old ways of thinking and acting. What was at stake in the conference was the very leading of the Holy Spirit and the very meaning of the gospel. There can be no doubt that the Holy Spirit was present and leading. The sense of love, courage, creativity, and energy which was felt by so many of the participants is clear testimony to this fact. The vast majority of those present left the conference energized to carry the faith back to their churches. Some present felt for the first time in their lives that they had been taken seriously as women. As a result they were liberated to own the faith fully for themselves. To imprison the gospel in the categories of the dominant male paradigms of the faith that have ruled the church for centuries would be a betrayal of the gospel. The gospel is a gospel of liberation which sets the victims free; hence to express the gospel in feminist and womanist terms is an act of profound faithfulness.

For critics to interpret what was said as heresy is itself heretical. Heresy is a tool which has systematically been used by the dominant oppressors and winners of theological wars to exclude those who are different and to control the reins of power. Moreover, it is idolatrous to imprison the gospel in some kind of orthodoxy, as if the mystery of the gospel can be captured in fixed language and doctrine. The gospel frees us from theological narrowness, intolerance, bigotry, and bondage. The conference itself was not a monolithic affair. Speakers and participants were free to disagree with one another so that they could represent accurately the diversity of suffering, experience, and oppression which was actually present in their lives. Expressing such diversity is not just important in its own right; it is also essential if the church is to take seriously the broadening of ecumenical vision which is now taking place across the worldwide church.

Finally, whatever other Christians may say by way of criticism, it is imperative that United Methodists remember that they have a unique calling to express a catholic spirit in their approach to ecumenical occasions. Such a spirit does not ask for uniformity in doctrine as a condition for fellowship and joint action. Even if there were some things said and done which were questionable to the orthodox, such a divergence from orthodoxy does not warrant withdrawal or opposition. United Methodists, following Wesley, are people who think and let think. If we can join together in heart, then we are to extend the hand of fellowship, provoking one another to love and good works. What matters in these circumstances is not unity in doctrine or belief, but unity in action and mission. Clearly

19

United Methodists are committed to the liberation of the oppressed, so that to stand aloof from the challenge of the conference because we do not agree with this or that component of what took place is a betrayal of our heritage. Moreover, the conference was in part an educational occasion where new questions never asked before in the church were creatively pursued, so that it is to be expected that some people would be upset, if not alarmed, by what was said. Our commitment to reason and persuasion commits us to the hazards of such dialogue and encounter.

THE CONCERNS OF THE CRITICS

Critics of the conference have a radically different interpretation and assessment of what was involved. Just as its defenders tend to place the events of the conference in a wider narrative, so too do its critics see the events as intimately related to other trends in the church as a whole. Their analysis runs something like this.

Most of the presentations at the conference, far from representing a revision of the Christian tradition, constituted the invention of a whole new post-Christian religion. Thus, the extended use of Sophia as the very name of God, over against the given Christian name of Father, Son, and Holy Spirit, is simply the tip of the iceberg of change envisaged. The very naming of the conference as an exercise in reimagining the whole spectrum of Christian doctrine and ethics from creation to sexual morality is a clear sign of deeper things at work. What is at stake is the rejection of essential Christian teaching and its replacement by a diverse smorgasbord of proposals which in a loose way add up to a whole new religion. Implicit in these proposals is a rejection of the Christian canon of scripture and its replacement by another canon informally stitched together from a widely diverse network of ancient and current sources. Insofar as the scriptures are used, or insofar as standard Christian doctrines and themes are deployed, they are used selectively to suit the new theology of the speakers, or they are artfully reworked to express the radical new ideas being introduced into the church.

In this new religion, salvation is from patriarchy rather than from sin; membership is secured not by grace but by being a victim of one kind or another; salvation is secured not by faith but through works of liberation. As this new religion has developed over the last twenty years, its proponents have systematically substituted their own inventions for the various components which form the content of the Christian faith. They have constructed their own hermeneutic of suspicion, rather than listening to the faith as grounded in divine revelation. They have developed their own kind of liturgical rites and ceremonies, hanging loose to or completely subverting the worship of the church. And they have now begun to articulate their own sources and modes of knowledge. Over time this new religion has cultivated its own patterns of biblical interpretation, its own forms of pastoral care, its own visions of apologetics, and its own characteristic suggestions about the nature of sexuality and ethics. Despite the diversity which can be discerned in the movements represented at the conference, there is in fact a significant web of unity which weaves the various elements together into a whole. This is a new religion where one gains entry by being a certain kind of victim, where one is saved by one's own efforts, where one gains knowledge of the divine not by special revelation but by special kinds of experience, and where the social outcome is a whole new community with its own liturgies, ecclesial practices, and boundaries.

The claim that this is in fact the work of the Holy Spirit is understandable but false. It is understandable because many are all too ready to identify the Holy Spirit as the cause of whatever brings new energy and enthusiasm into their spiritual lives. However, this is a precarious criterion for identifying the working of the Spirit. The relevant criterion of the work of the Spirit is to be located in the extent to which the purported activity brings glory and honor to Jesus Christ. In this instance, however, the place of Christ is entirely marginal. His life and work are treated as a disguise for other claims and convictions which function as the ultimate criterion of the work of the Spirit. Hence the claim to being guided by the Spirit is false.

In these circumstances it is entirely appropriate to speak of heresy, for these developments constitute a radical departure from the faith of the church over the centuries. These proposals are not an enrichment of the faith; they are a falling away from the faith. Moreover, these developments cannot be defended in the name of ecumenism, for essential to ecumenism is a commitment to the great verities of the apostolic tradition, which here are set aside either directly or indirectly. To argue that participation is to be defended on the grounds of the catholic spirit would be the equivalent of having John Wesley defend the participation of early Methodists in rallies to support the Deism or Socinianism of the eighteenth century, heresies he explicitly rejected in his day. Wesley vigorously opposed such departures from the faith, recognizing that they struck at the root of the great truths of the gospel. Nor can it be seriously argued that opposition to these new doctrines really constitutes opposition to the role of women in the ministry of theological reflection. On the contrary, the rightful place of women in the church and its intellectual life will be hurt when women are identified with proposals that undermine the whole fabric of the faith from within.

Finally, the development of this new faith should not come as a surprise to anyone acquainted with the history of mainline Protestant theology. For two centuries and more many of the intellectual elites of the tradition have been convinced that the historical faith of the church is untenable. Rejecting the possibility of special divine revelation enshrined in scripture, they have been forced to find an alternative justification for the radical revisions of Christian doctrine which are needed to replace the apostolic faith of the church. The favored alternative warrant has been that of experience and the favored alternative doctrinal vision has focused to a greater or lesser degree on transformation of the world more than the conversion and formation of Christian believers. Moreover, there has been a sustained attempt to treat premodern conceptions of the Christian tradition as failing to do justice to the sensibilities of "modern man."

The secular emancipation of women has been the cue for the developments which have dramatically appeared in the Reimagining Conference. However, the platform which made this possible was brilliantly constructed by the Liberal Protestants of the last two centuries. Shifting the focus from "modern men" to "modern women," the proponents of reimagining have attempted to develop a faith which is appropriate and credible to the intellectual norms now favored in the culture. Hence the development of the new religion envisaged is both a continuation and a radical departure from trends long at work.

The continuities with the Liberal Protestant experiment are visible in several ways. Both Liberal Protestants and the new reimaginers reject the view that there is a deposit of apostolic faith; both worry that any attempt to capture the tradition in specific doctrines is a form of idolatry; both are driven to revise the faith to fit changing circumstances; both view the Christian faith as directed primarily to the transformation of the world; both appeal to experience as the authority or warrant for doctrine. The discontinuities with Liberal Protestantism are also very visible. The reimaginers prefer to appeal to romantic and corporate conceptions of credibility; they reject intellectualist and rational conceptions of credibility; they worry that all forms of rationality can easily be the bearers of oppression and violence against women and minorities; and they accord a deep significance to liturgical activity in the church. The discontinuities are also visible in the place they give to emotion and silence in the life of faith, in their eagerness to overthrow politically the classical faith of the church because of its inherently patriarchal origins, and in their readiness to use ancient pagan or heretical material to reimagine the gospel for a new generation.

On this analysis the contents of the Reimagining Conference represent the radical extreme of a process which has long been at work in modern Protestantism. The reaction of shock and horror among ordinary Christians is, however, entirely understandable. It represents a doctrinal awakening which has been long delayed due to the dexterity of many church leaders in shielding their flocks from the consequences of theological revision in the tradition as a whole. Not surprisingly such leaders, including many bishops, are tempted to attack the critics of Reimagining as disloyal to United Methodism, for they expose a disciplinary vacuum which they themselves are loath to occupy, but which they are also reluctant to hand over to self-appointed watchdogs.

THE NEED FOR DOCTRINAL DISCUSSION

My aim in outlining these rather artificial descriptions and assessments of the Reimagining Conference has been modest. They make no pretense to be historically accurate. Indeed it is well nigh impossible to provide an accurate analysis of the protagonists at this stage, and I seriously doubt whether we could find a defender or a critic who holds the positions I have just constructed. Rather, my aim has been to try to capture the radically different sensibilities which the conference has evoked in the church as a whole.

As I weigh the materials and the responses, I detect a tragic dimension to the whole discussion. Equally well-informed and sincere people are convinced that what is at stake for them is the substance of the gospel, the working of the Holy Spirit, and the very core of their identity as Christians. Mature and sophisticated exponents of both views are also aware of this. In their better moments, they can recognize the absolute integrity of their opponents, even though they are well aware of the emotional, moral, and political currents which swirl like a tornado around the debate. Moreover, they are aware that it is highly unlikely that even the most astute and intellectually gifted will be able to persuade their best opponents to change their minds.

Precisely because the debate cuts this deeply, we are reluctant to face the fact that there is a real either/or to be identified and worked through. The differences at stake here cannot be smoothed over or gotten rid of by appeals for reconciliation, or by requests for better exercises in communication, or by calls for more piety and goodwill all around. These kinds of moves are understandable, but they will not work. If anything, they will only add to the frustration which already abounds. Nor can the differences be resolved by insisting that this is just one more internal dispute about how to interpret this or that component in the faith, such as is common throughout Christian history. Even when this judgment is made by informed bishops, such a posture merely postpones the inevitable. This dispute cuts to the very identity of the gospel and the faith. Soothing words accompanied by pious smiles will no longer suffice to deal with the problem. It is this fact that explains the depth and anger which have surfaced on various sides in this debate.

The same point can be made by saying that in the end the debate is a doctrinal debate. It is focused on the doctrinal content and identity of the Christian tradition. Both sides claim to be enacting the substance of the Christian heritage in their judgments. This is patently visible in the way they outline their assessments. Yet the alternative assessments cannot both be correct. They are profoundly incompatible with each other. There are, of course, those who would love to smooth things over, saying that both can welcome each other into the same family to work side by side in mission and ministry. Yet this case is impossible to sustain. The differences concern the very identity and boundaries of the Christian tradition itself. Action and mission will be entirely different depending on which construal of the faith is being deployed. The liberal appeal to stop fussing and get on with transforming the world no longer rings true in this situation; in fact, it is a hopelessly hollow and superficial response to the predicament.

SECURING OUR BEARINGS IN THE DEBATE

As we ponder the significance of this kind of disagreement, I suggest that two points be kept in mind.

First, there is an interesting parallel between this kind of dispute and that which emerged in the first four centuries of the Christian tradition. The early church took time to work out its canonical traditions. Initially it focused on survival and evangelistic expansion, although from the beginning, as we can see in many of the later epistles of the New Testament, there was a lively awareness of the significance of doctrinal boundaries. As the church succeeded in its evangelistic work and became more secure in the hostile environment of the Roman Empire, it had to face questions about the core of its message and of its identity. The pressures on this core were both internal and external. Insiders raised deep questions about the meaning and significance of Jesus Christ and outsiders forced the church to explain its faith. Moreover, one of the perennial problems Christianity had to resolve was how to relate to the secular teaching of the day. Should it reject such teaching entirely? Should it accept secular learning and express the faith in terms of the prevailing convictions of the day? Or should it borrow very carefully and only use such foreign material as could be legitimately baptized and transformed for use in the service of divine revelation? Resolving such questions was a painful and complicated exercise.

Likewise, United Methodism is, comparatively speaking, a very young church. It is only now entering its third century of service. Rather than being in European terms a dying remnant of the old Christendom, it is really one of the younger churches facing precisely the kind of challenge which is common among ecclesiastical adolescents. It is this which accounts for the lively and volatile dimensions of the current debate. It also accounts for the focus on the interaction with the surrounding culture. What is going on, therefore, is the natural outcome for a tradition which has gotten beyond its initial evangelistic phase and must now sort out its fundamental identity. The stakes in this kind of debate are indeed high, as the parallel with the second and third centuries makes clear. Decisions made at this point in history will have lasting consequences for generations to come. That is surely one reason why it is not enough to muddle through and hope for the best.

Second, while the parallel with the early church holds, it must not be pressed too far. Although United Methodism is now engaged in a deep, informal debate about its identity, this is not the first time it has confronted the matter. In fact, the Methodist movement had to face the question of its doctrinal identity very early on when it migrated from Ireland and England to the New World. At that time Methodism resolved the matter very deliberately, but then it immediately set forth on its massive efforts in evangelization. Perhaps it never really spent enough time working through questions of identity in the first place. Not surprisingly, many have forgotten this earlier debate and have wanted to resolve the fundamental disputes by starting from scratch. For better or worse, this cannot be done. Decisions were made early on; these cannot be undone with the stroke of a pen, or by wishful thinking which walks away from history.

It is at this juncture that appeal to relevant evidence is absolutely pivotal. My argument in what follows is that we can settle the question of the doctrinal identity of United Methodism clearly and definitively. Just as the early church settled these matters in early councils, so Methodism settled these matters in its General Conferences. United Methodism really does have a set of doctrinal standards which can now be clearly identified. To argue otherwise is to turn history on its head and to opt for some kind of doctrinal and theological obscurantism which cannot credibly be sustained. This is a very hard lesson for modern United Methodists to learn, for, at the crucial moment when they have to face the truth, they readily cave in to pious sentimentality and romantic improvisation. Facing the truth is the only way to freedom for everyone.

Given this analysis, the current flap about the Reimagining Conference is something of a sideshow. It would be quite false to say that it is insignificant. It is an unintended confrontation which caught many off guard and exposes a fissure that has long been lurking beneath the surface. However, the debate surrounding this conference will continue to swirl around such questions as, What actually happened? Who really said what and what did it signify? Who is allowed to do what in the agencies and boards of the church? We can all add our own list of questions.

This debate, however, merely raises the curtain on deeper issues. The really crucial question is the logically prior question about United Methodist doctrinal standards, which I have already raised. Does United Methodism have any doctrines constitutive of its identity? And if it does, can these be identified? Sooner or later these matters will have to be addressed, if we are to make any substantial progress in tackling problems of unity and disunity. The good news is that these questions can be answered unequivocally. They admit of clear adjudication on the basis of substantial evidence and argument. There is no need for emotional panic or despair.

Yet we must proceed patiently. As I have already indicated, the problem of doctrinal disunity is only one of a host of difficulties that have surfaced of late within United Methodism. Putting the matter more positively, it is no accident that amidst much talk about difficulties of one sort or another, there is also much yearning for renewal. In fact, I am convinced that United Methodism in its own way is undergoing profound renewal. Those internal and external critics who have written off the tradition are premature in their judgments. It is not just that there are thriving local congregations, faithfully and creatively serving the Lord. There are all sorts of signs that the tradition is coming to terms with its problems and genuinely seeking a fresh baptism of the Holy Spirit.

What has not been noticed, however, is that there is a clear link between general spiritual renewal in the church and the renewal of Christian doctrine. Indeed, without the healing effects of the deep truths of the Christian faith, any renewal will be superficial and short-lived. The current debate about doctrine is, therefore, a providential development, inviting the whole church to find a deeper way to be healed by the Holy Spirit. Good doctrine, properly received, is like an effective medicine which will work wonders in the church. Of course, if doctrine becomes simply a weapon of war, we can all predict the consequences. It will be like drinking hemlock; it will kill us spiritually and intellectually. Hence pursuing this whole matter in the right tone and in the right manner is pivotal for the ultimate outcome. In this arena we have really no alternative other than to pursue the discussion in fear and trembling before God.

The current search for renewal involves diagnoses and prescriptions of what has gone wrong in the church that are inescapably doctrinal in two ways. First, they are doctrinal in that the very identifications of what has gone wrong and how to put things right have clear doctrinal overtones. One cannot say what is wrong and how to put it right without doctrinal commitments. Second, they are doctrinal because many of the problems currently debated have clear doctrinal roots. They stem from doctrinal aberration of a very particular sort.

This is another reason why it would be a mistake to focus on the Reimagining Conference. Both sides in the debate are right to say that pivotal issues are at stake. They are wrong, however, if they think that this is the only place where doctrinal debate arises. Doctrinal matters are at stake elsewhere in the church's life. In fact, they crop up all over the place for those who have eyes to see. Hence it is only as we seek delicately to chart these other areas that we will be able to see the deep significance of the central thesis I shall present up ahead. Our immediate concern in the next two chapters is to chart the debate about doctrine in United Methodism over the last twenty years or so. With that in place we shall relate our conclusions about that debate to the wider search of renewal which we all so gladly desire as a gift of the Holy Spirit in the whole Church of Jesus Christ.

Chapter Two

The Quest for Doctrinal Standards

THE ORIGINS OF THE QUEST

Over the last twenty years United Methodists have found themselves facing questions about doctrine such as have rarely been seen by a modern mainline Protestant denomination. At least three factors have fed this flurry of intellectual activity. There was first the creation of United Methodism as a new denomination. The creation of United Methodism in 1968 forced its leaders to work out how to bring together two streams of the Wesleyan tradition without violating the respective constitutions of the merging churches. Perhaps for the first time in two centuries, Wesleyan leaders had to think very seriously about the clauses in their traditions which insisted that Methodists, contrary to their own well-worn avowals, really did have confessional commitments buried in their origins and patently visible in their constitutions.

Second, after the merger United Methodists found themselves forced to deal in a profound way with deep uncertainty about their own doctrinal identity. On the one side they clearly were committed to certain doctrinal standards. The First Restrictive Rule of the Constitution (Section III) clearly stated this to be the case. It reads: "The General Conference shall not revoke, alter, or change our Articles of Religion or establish any new standards or rules of doctrine contrary to our present existing and established standards of doctrine." On the other hand, nobody seemed to know

31

what these standards were. Nor was there a clear view as to what should be done with these doctrinal standards, were they to be clearly identified. Thus it was only fitting that a doctrinal commission should be set up to resolve these and other matters when the new denomination was founded.

The report of this commission constitutes the third reason for extensive United Methodist attention to its doctrinal identity. What was intended to settle matters for the next century or more really became the occasion for further discussion and debate. I vividly remember talking this over with Albert Outler, the crucial architect of the 1972 report, while he was giving a set of lectures at Seattle Pacific University. He made it very clear that he expected the report of 1972 to serve the church for at least another two hundred years before it would need to be revisited.

Everyone was taken by surprise, then, when Richard Heitzenrater, one of the finest historians produced by the tradition in recent years, argued a novel proposal on the historical identity of the doctrinal standards as posited by the First Restrictive Rule. Heitzenrater went so far as to claim that early Methodism refused to adopt the writings of Wesley in his *Sermons* and *Explanatory Notes on the New Testament* as its doctrinal standards. This caused a firestorm for a while. When the dust finally settled after a report was brought to the General Conference of 1988, United Methodists returned to their dogmatic slumbers. For most people it was difficult to muster much interest in the debate. Indeed, it is extremely difficult to find a United Methodist who can provide even a rudimentary narrative of what took place at the General Conference of 1988.

Despite such indifference, doctrinal questions will not go away; they keep resurfacing here and there. Thus the recent decision of General Conference to add a clause holding bishops responsible for guarding the doctrinal heritage of the church has led to questions as to what exactly that heritage is and how it may be guarded. According to the *Book of Discipline* (1992), the bishops are "to guard, transmit, teach, and proclaim, corporately and individually, the apostolic faith as it is expressed in Scripture and Tradition, and, as they are led and endowed by the Spirit, to interpret that faith evangelically and prophetically" (par. 514.2). Furthermore, as we have noted already, the Reimagining Conference has led to informal charges of heresy, which in turn have been met with sharp rebuttals from various leaders in agencies connected with the conference and more generally in the church.

Moreover, from time to time Boards of Ordained Ministry have been forced to grapple with the content of United Methodist doctrine in their work of examining candidates for the ordained ministry. I recently met one chairperson of a Board of Ordained Ministry who had become deeply concerned because the criteria of assessment they were using in his board tended to exclude candidates who held traditional Christian views concerning the Trinity and the place of Jesus Christ in the salvation of the world. In another case, I encountered a seminary student who was not permitted to proceed to ordination as deacon in part because she rejected certain feminist conceptions of God on the grounds that they were modalistic rather than trinitarian. Clearly it is in this domain, that is, in the domain of doctrinal oversight of candidates for the ministry, that United Methodism faces its biggest challenge, for it is in the Boards of Ordained Ministry that the church officially and regularly faces questions about its doctrinal identity. Moreover, it is the clergy whom they approve who will in practice bear the heaviest share of the task of teaching the faith in the church.

In this chapter I have three aims. First, I want to provide a normative account of the term "United Methodist Doctrine." I shall argue a case as to how United Methodist doctrine and doctrinal standards should be identified. Second, I shall provide a brief analysis of the function of doctrine or doctrinal standards in Methodism. Third, I shall attempt to provide a narrative of the developments from 1968 up to the present. Within this I shall suggest that the decisions of the General Conference of 1988 are both substantial and ingenious. I shall finish by identifying some of the challenges which my overall analysis implies for the church.

THE MEANING OF "UNITED METHODIST DOCTRINE"

By the term "United Methodist Doctrine," I mean that body of doctrine which The United Methodist Church has legislatively designated as its formal standards of doctrine. The warrant for this claim is simple: It is only the General Conference of The United Methodist Church which can actually speak for the church as a whole. This does not mean that a General Conference is free to do whatever it likes in the domain of doctrine. A General Conference must abide by its own constitution and the carefully crafted restrictive rules that bind its current action. No individual member, no presbyter, no bishop or group of bishops, no agency or commission can speak for and represent the church as a whole. Only the General Conference can do this. Contrary to what is often thought in popular circles, the term "United Methodist Doctrine" does not, therefore, refer to the doctrines which any particular United Methodist, or group of United Methodists, or even the whole of United Methodism itself, might contingently hold at any point in its history, as determined, say, by sociological or historical inquiry. Christians of all denominations are, of course, often woefully ignorant of the doctrines normatively held by their church. However, this is beside the point. The referent for the term "United Methodist Doctrine" is not sociological but broadly constitutional. It refers to those doctrines formally adopted by The United Methodist Church, acting in its legislative capacity, and thus endowed with the power to speak normatively, canonically, and officially.

So likewise the term "United Methodist Doctrine" does not refer to the doctrines or theological proposals actually held or argued for by theologians, professional or otherwise, who happen to have been or now are United Methodists. In North America, United Methodism has produced its own cadre of theologians; one thinks immediately of figures like Georgia Harkness, Edwin Lewis, Albert Outler, John Deschner, Thomas Langford, Justo González, Schubert Ogden, Thomas Oden, and Rebecca Chopp. One might even argue, as Thomas Langford has done, that there is a distinctive Wesleyan theological tradition with its own unique theme or themes, its own specific ethos, and its own distinctive methodology.[1] Yet again, this is not what we mean when we speak of "United Methodist Doctrine." We mean by this term those doctrines which have become canonical for the church as a whole; those teachings which have been voted on in the appropriate General Conference; that body of doctrinal material which has been formally adopted by the church through appropriate action in its courts.

It is easy to overlook this. Consider the following comment by Edward W. Poitras.

Religious traditions show great veneration for their founders. The Protestant family of Christian groups is no exception, for almost all of them have early founders or leaders whose life and thought are influential, even normative for their communities' lives. The Methodists follow this pattern, but are even more dependent than most Protestants upon their founder in that *they have no set of traditionally authorized creedal affirmations,* so find themselves driven to analyze the career and writings of John Wesley for some kind of authoritative standard to guide their development.

35

That Poitras himself is wary of this generalization is borne
out by the qualifications which follow immediately.

> There have been Methodist statements of faith, to be sure,
> such as the doctrinal summaries recorded in the early Meth-
> odist Annual Conference Minutes and later affirmations
> from the North American and other Methodist communi-
> ties, but the early ones were sketchy and most of them have
> never been accepted with the authority ascribed to such
> definitions as the Westminster Confession, Lutheran confes-
> sions and catechisms, or the Anglican Articles.[2]

Poitras' essay may well be a fine summary of "authentic
Wesleyanism." It certainly deserves to be taken seriously as
a contribution to that debate, but as a potential substitute for
the actual doctrinal standards adopted by the Methodist
tradition in North America it is on the wrong track. Moreover, the second quotation is incompatible with the claims
of the first. As he points out in the second quotation given
here, Protestant groups do have creedal affirmations.
United Methodism is no exception, and there is nothing
sketchy about them. What makes Methodism different is
that it has *also* used Wesley's *Sermons* and *Explanatory Notes
on the New Testament* as doctrinal standards. Important
though the life of Wesley is for United Methodism, it does
not count as a doctrinal standard in any shape or form.

All this is not to say that the work of a United Methodist
theologian might not become normative. In fact in 1972 The
United Methodist Church came within a hairsbreadth of
making both the doctrines and the theological methodology
of Albert Outler normative for the tradition. Even now this
issue is not yet resolved in the minds of many members of
the church, as we shall see in our next chapter, when we look
at the interpretation of the doctrinal standards of The United
Methodist Church over the last generation. In actual fact,
however, it is very difficult for theologians to get their work

accepted as normative in United Methodism. To achieve this status the work of an individual theologian or group of theologians has to be officially adopted and endorsed in an appropriate way by the General Conference. Thus it has to meet certain stringent constitutional requirements which are well nigh impossible to satisfy. What this reveals is that there is a clear, logical distinction between standards of doctrine accepted as canonical for United Methodism and the doctrines and theology of this or that theologian or group of theologians within United Methodism.

The general failure to observe this distinction has led to enormous confusion in the church. The doctrinal commitments of favored theologians, who happen to be United Methodist, are taken as constituting the doctrinal commitments of the church. Their membership in The United Methodist Church is taken in these circumstances as a warrant for identifying their doctrines as the doctrines of The United Methodist Church. Given that the theologians who are picked out in this process generally differ very radically from one another, it should come as no surprise that people think the church as a whole has collapsed into doctrinal chaos. The chaos among the theologians is construed as a fundamental, constitutional chaos. However, this is a case of mistaken identification. It is the General Conference, not any theologian or group of theologians, that speaks for the church. We will make no progress until we come to terms with this fact.

THE NEED FOR DOCTRINAL STANDARDS

Why do churches, including the early Methodist Church and its sister bodies, develop standards of doctrine? There are clearly a host of reasons, and we can readily identify why early Methodists did so in the eighteenth and nineteenth centuries. Broadly the reasons are human, social, pastoral, and evangelistic. Human beings, both corporately and individually, are very naturally driven to articulate those convictions which form and shape their lives. At a deep level intellectually, we are agents who need to put the insights and ideas that really matter to us into relatively comprehensive systems of teaching. Socially, we are forced by circumstances to explain our corporate identity to friends and foe. One way to do this is to draw up doctrinal summaries which explain who we are and what we believe. Pastorally, doctrinal schemes provide road maps for sorting out who we are, how our lives are made whole, and how we are to live in the world. In this respect they provide a pivotal role in preaching, pastoral care, and spiritual direction. Finally, for evangelism doctrinal proposals spell out the content of the gospel and the rudiments of basic teaching which are passed on to a new generation of Christian children and converts. Thus evangelism depends for its execution on convictions about creation, human nature, sin, salvation, and the like.

More generally evangelism depends on some understanding of what the gospel is. As Bonhoeffer so astutely observed, a church that loses its sense of the content of the gospel is much worse off than a church that goes morally astray. "False doctrine corrupts the life of the church at its source, and that is why doctrinal sin is more serious than moral. Those who rob the church of the gospel deserve the ultimate penalty, whereas those who fail in morality have the gospel there to help them."[3] This is a harsh judgment, but it is very perceptive. For the loss of the gospel means in the end that there is no hope for such a body. Moral failure and disaster are precisely what the gospel addresses and ultimately cures; so a church that is without the gospel has no medicine for its moral sickness; whereas a church that still has the gospel buried deep within its doctrinal standards and commitments always possesses grounds for hope. *Ipso facto* a church that has a healing word for its own sickness can reach out with a word of hope to outsiders. I am assuming here that it is not possible to spell out what the gospel is without adopting some body of Christian doctrine. I reject the facile notion that we could even conceive of the gospel without invoking one doctrine or another.

There are a host of reasons, then, why churches develop official or established standards of doctrine. Making such a move is not a fall into dead orthodoxy or a barren institutionalism. In fact, not nearly enough attention has been given to the manifold functions of doctrinal standards. It is common among recent commentators on standards of doctrine to focus almost exclusively on standards of doctrine as a means of identity across the generations.[4] This is important but clearly not the whole story. Standards of doctrine serve many functions. Beyond the functions already formally mentioned here, they help keep a body protected from subversive teaching, they provide means of evaluating leaders, they form part of the boundary to determine who is out and who is in, they act as a catalyst for continuing reflection, they are a crucial ingredient in ecumenical dialogue, they operate as a banner of conviction or a counsel of perfection, and they prevent bodies from falling into unhealthy extremes.

In broad terms standards of doctrine identify those convictions which a particular body has found invaluable if not essential to its existence; they provide a deep set of conceptual foundations in which a church can root and inform its ministry, its worship, its experience of God, its service to the world, and its internal discipline. A church can lay out its standards of doctrine in two ways: first, by actually specifying those teachings which it considers constitutive of its identity and existence; and second, by identifying the norm or norms against which its doctrines have been and are to be tested. The former method is more direct: It spells out those convictions about God, creation, sin, and the like which inform the church's life and hence its evangelistic life. The latter method is indirect, inviting continual reflection on the sources and grounds of the first order doctrines adopted; in the Protestant traditions it is usual to identify the scriptures as the ultimate source and norm of doctrine.

On this reading, standards of doctrine have a thoroughly complex character. They are obviously open to all sorts of abuse when their varied functions are misunderstood or wrongly applied. They can be used to impose limits to the freedom of the individual and even to the church as a whole in the long run; they can function to hamper commitment to deep theological reflection and creativity; they can become irrelevant and disconnected from real life; and they can be used as weapons in religious wars. We are all aware of the catalog of evils generally associated with doctrinal standards. The solution to these evils is not to abandon doctrinal standards; this is myopic and naive. The solution is to understand them more fully and more positively and to use them more deftly and more creatively.

FACING CONFUSION

This is precisely the challenge that faces The United Methodist Church in the present generation. We will not be able to meet it, however, without a review of the work of the last generation in its interpretation of the doctrinal standards in The United Methodist Church.

Developments in the interpretation of the doctrinal standards of The United Methodist Church over the last twenty years have been extraordinary. For nothing less than one hundred and sixty years the forebears of the United Methodists had not formally given serious attention to their doctrinal standards. So much so that by the late 1960s those who later became United Methodists were not able to identify with certainty what the standards were, or how they were to be construed and used. The issue was compounded by the clear statement in the First Restrictive Rule that United Methodism did have doctrinal standards which cannot be changed. On the surface this confusion bespoke a thoroughly incoherent ecclesial tradition; the church had doctrinal standards but no one knew for certain what they were. Under the surface it made manifest a deep set of dilemmas some of which still remain to be resolved.

At one level the confusion concerning doctrinal standards made manifest the incongruity between the constitution of the church and the general avowals of United Methodists. The common perception of United Methodists in the twentieth century has been that United Methodists believe anything they like. United Methodists have gloried in their lack of doctrinal unity, priding themselves, for example, that, unlike Presbyterians with their *Westminster Confession of Faith,* they do not belong to a creedal church.

This is a bizarre judgment. It utterly fails to jibe with the possession of a set of Articles of Religion, a Confession of Faith, and a First Restrictive Rule in the constitution of the church. However unlike other ecclesial bodies the forebears of United Methodism may have been, this kind of contrast is inept and inaccurate. It simply does not fit the historical record.

Nor does it fit the common practice among United Methodists to make much of such doctrinal themes as prevenient grace or the catholic spirit. Albert Outler rendered invaluable service to the church in insisting again and again that the doctrine of prevenient grace was a pivotal feature of teaching in the Methodist tradition. When this and other doctrines like justification by faith, or the witness of the Holy Spirit in assurance, are construed as essential doctrine of The United Methodist Church, the whole attempt to argue that United Methodism does not have doctrines must be immediately abandoned.

At another level the confusion about doctrinal standards drew attention to the question of how United Methodism intended to relate its own distinctive doctrinal heritage, as highlighted in the writings of Wesley, to the wider heritage of the Christian tradition. This question was made particularly acute because of the deep ecumenical impulse in the Wesleyan tradition. Once we moved beyond our ecclesial ghettos, we were forced to deal with our relationship to the common doctrinal heritage of the church. We had to raise and try to resolve the wider issue of the center of gravity in doctrine in the church universal. Was it to be located, say, in one's doctrine of God, or in the material of the ecumenical creeds, or in the doctrine of salvation, as worked out by Wesley? Where was the core of our doctrine to be located and why? Without answers to these kinds of questions it is difficult to enter into serious ecumenical dialogue.

At another level the confusion about doctrinal standards brought to light the thorny issue of the warrant of specific doctrines. To what authority, if any, were we committed? How far was this matter of criteria for doctrine in fact addressed in those documents which might plausibly be construed as the doctrinal standards? Should United Methodism be seen as fundamentally a Protestant body, a proposal supported by the generally Protestant content and tenor of several articles and by sundry material in Wesley's *Sermons?* Or should United Methodism be seen as more a Catholic body, a construal supported by the concentration of material from the early centuries in the Articles and Confession, and by the appeal to tradition in Wesley's *Sermons?* Or should United Methodism be seen as offering a hybrid of Christian and Enlightenment traditions, an interpretation suggested by the scanty and unorganized references to scripture, tradition, experience, and reason?

At yet another level all the confusion about doctrinal standards inherent in the late sixties and early seventies raised the question of how any Christian body that had roots extending back before the Enlightenment could come to terms with the challenges of modernity. Could Methodism maintain both its fundamental intellectual identity and its continuing relevance and credibility at the same time? It is very tempting to believe that the fog which hit the church arose precisely because many leaders and intellectuals were convinced that the actual doctrines officially held by the church were simply incredible, and that the way to avoid facing the uncomfortable consequences of this was to suggest that the church really did not have any doctrines.

Certainly, Methodism has from within its own womb given birth to a variety of doctrinal and theological strategies which in one way or another have attempted to face up to the intellectual needs of its members and its changing context.[5] United Methodism was from the start deeply enculturated. Its leaders prided themselves in lauding many of the values, like freedom, autonomy, and critical rationality, which were some of the benchmarks of modernity. Moreover, its intellectual leaders also acutely felt the tension, which the Enlightenment celebrated and emphasized, between the intellectual commitments of the classical Christian tradition and the perceived demands of much modern theorizing about history and the world.[6] This precipitated a quest for an identity which would be not just doctrinal but theological in nature. That is to say, it called for an account of how United Methodism conceived its own theological task in the modern world. If there was one problem which lay at the root of the confusion among United Methodists in the early seventies, then this is surely a likely candidate.

A FIRST ATTEMPT AT RESOLUTION

Given such a complex set of dilemmas it will come as no surprise that different interpretations of what happened at the General Conference of 1972 abound. As I see it, what happened was this.

1. The query about what constituted the doctrinal standards was resolved by identifying these clearly as the *Articles of Religion,* the *Confession of Faith,* and Wesley's *Sermons* and *Explanatory Notes on the New Testament.*[7] Their authority, however, was eviscerated by treating them as strictly nonjuridical, as landmarks in our complex historical heritage, as foundation documents which were subject to historical interpretation, and as radically contextualized in a one-sided version of the view that no language could ever really describe God at all. In other words, after the standards were identified, they were immediately undercut by being construed as lacking in effective force in the life of the church. They were lost in a sea of relativistic assumptions.

2. This way of identifying the status of the doctrinal standards provided the context for resolving the problem of the relation between the classical tradition of Christendom and the Wesleyan emphasis. It was solved by insisting on a common core and a set of United Methodist distinctive beliefs. Presumably this simply specified in a nuanced way the essential doctrinal content of the standards.[8] However, as this material was subject to the relativistic assumptions just mentioned, the effect of identifying the content of the standards in this way was to render them null and void.

3. The question of authority was resolved by means of the famous Methodist quadrilateral.[9] Scripture, tradition, reason, and experience were recommended as the doctrinal guidelines of The United Methodist Church.[10] Within this an effort was made to do two things: first, to specify the content of tradition, and second, to develop a working account of the relation among the four elements. Yet the guidelines were so broad that the quadrilateral provided for

the equivalent of a lateral pass in football: If you cannot get what you desire on one ground, pass laterally to the next until you do.

4. This last move on authority provided the leverage for resolving the tension between past doctrinal identity and current theological reflection and expression. This was the crux of the matter in the end. The primacy clearly belonged to continuing theological reflection. United Methodist identity was to be secured by the way in which one did theology rather than by what one believed doctrinally. Process took precedence over content. United Methodist identity was located not in the content of what one believed but in the process of how one came to believe. As a consequence, or even as constitutive of this, United Methodism embraced a radical doctrinal pluralism as its way of life doctrinally. It is fascinating that after 1968 the *Doctrines and Discipline* becomes merely the *Book of Discipline*. It is difficult to imagine a more telling symbol of the deep shift which took place among United Methodists. We might accurately summarize the situation in this way. What made one a United Methodist from a doctrinal point of view was a clear commitment to developing those doctrines which could be supported in an appropriate way by scripture, tradition, reason, and experience.

The crucial shift is nicely captured in the following section of the *Discipline*.

Since "our present existing and established standards of doctrine" cited in the first two Restrictive Rules of the Constitution of The United Methodist Church are not to be construed literally and juridically, then by what methods can our doctrinal reflection and construction be most fruitful and fulfilling? The answer comes in terms of our free inquiry within the boundaries defined by four main sources and guidelines for Christian theology: Scripture, tradition, experience, reason. These four are interdependent; none can be

45

defined unambiguously. They allow for, indeed they positively encourage, variety in United Methodist theologizing. Jointly, they have provided a broad and stable context for reflection and formulation. Interpreted with appropriate flexibility, self-discipline, and prayer, they may instruct us as we carry forward our never-ending tasks of theologizing in The United Methodist Church.[11]

RADICAL REAPPRAISAL AND RESOLUTION

If the construction of this proposal was intrinsically extraordinary, that is, it involved the location of identity ultimately in the adoption of a complex theological method, its radical reappraisal within the space of twenty years was even more so. Again I can only touch on the crucial highlights.

Ostensibly what the 1988· General Conference did was tidy up the material from the decisions of 1972. It adopted a diplomatic style by trying to change the direction without appearing to do so in a radical way. Thus it made more explicit the basic Christian affirmations shared with other churches. Likewise, it tidied up the content of the distinctive Wesleyan emphases. Despite the fact that this appears more as clarification than substantial change, the difference here is enormous, for now identity is shifting back from method to doctrinal substance.

At another level the proposals brought to the General Conference sorted out the much-debated question of the referent for our "present existing and established standards of doctrine."[12]

This could have been a nightmare to resolve, in that there developed a crisis for the church when it was argued forcefully by Richard Heitzenrater that these did not at all refer to Wesley's *Sermons* and *Notes* but rather to the *Articles of Religion*.[13] Heitzenrater's claim is that up until 1784, while American Methodism was part of British Methodism, the doctrinal standards were constituted by the *Sermons* and *Notes*. In 1784 a separate organization was established and thereafter the *Sermons* and *Notes* did not have the status of doctrinal standards. The new *Discipline* adopted did not specify any doctrinal standards, but it was clear from those sections which addressed the issue of doctrinal discipline that the standard used to test doctrinal orthodoxy was that of the revised articles sent over by Wesley. This position was officially ratified by the General Conference of 1808, when action was taken to regulate and perpetuate the General Conference and the First Restrictive Rule was adopted. After the passing of the Rule, an attempt was made by Francis Ward to have the *Sermons* and *Notes,* together with other writings, be identified in a memorandum of understanding as containing the principal doctrines of Methodism. Ward's motion lost, indicating the *rejection* of the *Sermons* and *Notes* as the doctrinal standards of Methodism. That coveted position went to the *Articles of Religion.* Moreover, Ward's motion was deliberately struck from the *Journal,* hiding from the printed record what had actually happened in the conference. Not knowing what had happened, mid-nineteenth-century bishops and leaders gradually began to bring back in the *Sermons* and *Notes,* thereby preparing the way for the kind of confusion which was to engulf the church a century later.

Heitzenrater's proposal was a bombshell, for all along, whatever might be said in favor of the Methodist quadrilateral, it was generally agreed that the *Sermons* and *Notes* had at least some connection to the doctrinal standards of the Methodist movement, a position vigorously articulated and defended by Thomas Oden.[14] The crux of his argument was that from the beginning it was agreed and known within Methodism that the standards were not limited to the Articles but included also the *Sermons* and *Notes.* In fact the Articles were simply added to the already adopted *Sermons* and *Notes;* in turn the Articles were used in cases of trial for doctrinal aberration. Moreover, the very wording of the First Restrictive Rule in terms of dual clauses points to two sets of texts and not just to one set of articles. Hence the whole attempt to reject the *Sermons* and *Notes* is a misreading of the situation in early American Methodism. The silence on the *Sermons* and *Notes* was really an indication of confidence and moral certainty which assumed that everyone knew they were the present and established standards of doctrine.

Clearly this deep historical disagreement could very easily have derailed any attempt to arrive at a solution of the problem of what constitutes the doctrines of The United Methodist Church. What is the church to do when its scholars are at loggerheads on fundamental matters of historical fact and interpretation? The solution adopted at the General Conference was a stroke of ecclesiastical genius: the *Sermons* and *Notes* were treated as *de jure* canonical but made *de facto* subsidiary to the *Articles of Religion* and *Confession of Faith.* In other words, the solution was to include all the disputed material but recognize that the *Sermons* and *Notes* were a subsidiary extension of the primary material contained in the *Articles of Religion* and the *Confession of Faith.*[15] This was an extraordinarily astute decision, one which is subtle and sensitive enough to restore one's faith in the working of the Holy Spirit in the courts of the church. Some are utterly convinced that the outcome was as much due to extensive intercessory prayer behind the scenes as it was to any merely human effort.

The crucial argument which may well have resolved the historical logjam was the claim that the formation of The United Methodist Church actually took place in 1968. At that point a whole new church was formed. In the Plan of Union that led to the formation of The United Methodist Church, it was clear that Wesley's *Sermons* and *Notes* were already identified as included in the doctrinal standards. Hence to exclude them in 1988 would have meant a repudiation of the founding documents of the new church. In this way the whole question of what happened back in 1808 could be left on one side.[16] In other words, to leave out the *Sermons* and *Notes* could well have precipitated an even deeper constitutional crisis than the one the members of the General Conference already had on their hands.

Furthermore, the Conference action of 1988 cleared up the vexed question of the primacy of scripture, making what was implicit much more explicit, while retaining a commitment to tradition, reason, and experience. "United Methodists share with other Christians the conviction that Scripture is the primary source and criterion for Christian doctrine."[17] Tradition, experience, and reason are described in such a way as to safeguard this primacy. "In theological reflection, the resources of tradition, experience, and reason are integral to our study of Scripture without displacing Scripture's primacy for faith and practice."[18]

In addition the Conference retained the challenge to engage in continuing doctrinal and theological reflection which would attend to the concerns generated by various human struggles for dignity, liberation, and fulfillment, by various ethnic constituencies, by the praxis of mission and ministry, and by ecumenical and interfaith dialogue. Within this call to theological reflection an attempt was made to chart a clear distinction between doctrine and theology. The doctrinal affirmations assist in the discernment of Christian truth in ever-changing circumstances, while theology includes the testing, renewal, elaboration, and application of our doctrinal perspective.[19]

Clearly all these complex developments contributed in their own way to removing the suspicion that United Methodists had opted for doctrinal indifference when they embraced an identity that focused primarily on the method or process of doing theology, rather than on any doctrinal consensus. Doctrinal indifference was countered by being much clearer about the role of the *Articles of Religion,* the *Confession of Faith,* and the *Sermons* and *Notes,* by making more explicit the relation between scripture and the other three elements of the quadrilateral, by dropping all talk of doctrinal or theological pluralism,[20] and by insisting on a distinction between doctrine and theology. All this is to my mind an enormous gain. It leaves United Methodism doctrinally in a much healthier condition than it was in the late sixties. In fact I think that constitutionally United Methodism is in extremely good shape as it moves into a new century of service to God and the world. The fog which engulfed the church in the late sixties and early seventies is now gone. United Methodists can now be clear about their doctrinal identity. That identity is constituted by the church's *Articles of Religion* and *Confession of Faith,* material which gives it the common faith of the church universal, and by Wesley's *Sermons* and *Notes,* material which spells out the distinctives of its own unique appropriation of the gospel in its formative period.

However, constitutional health is a meager affair if the constitution of the church on doctrinal matters is not known, or if it is forgotten, if it is systematically ignored, or if it is otherwise set aside. The challenges facing The United Methodist Church in the light of the argument presented here are clear. Can United Methodists identify the content of their doctrines and their doctrinal standards? Does United Methodism really accept its own doctrines? Does it take them seriously in its work and ministry? Does it know how to teach them across the generations? Does it know how to interpret them and relate them to new situations? Does it have ways of ensuring that the teachers of the tradition, most especially the presbyters, are really committed to the doctrinal standards of the church? Does it have ways of ensuring that its overseers and guardians of the tradition, namely, its bishops, both own the tradition and hold themselves and the church as a whole accountable to these traditions? It is these challenges which I shall now attempt to address.

Chapter Three

The Search for Doctrinal Identity

THE POPULAR PICTURE OF DOCTRINE

Some years ago a theologian friend of mine, who had just come back from a long spell of study in Germany and who had decided on theological grounds to become a United Methodist, joined First United Methodist Church in Dallas. Naturally he and his family very quickly became part of one of the Sunday school classes. On one of their first days in the class they were greeted by one of the members, who had transferred some years before from the Southern Baptist tradition. The rationale for transferring to The United Methodist Church was simple. Where before, as Southern Baptists, they had to accept a whole system of doctrine, they were now free, as United Methodists, to believe anything they liked.

I do not think that it is an exaggeration to claim that this sort of story could be repeated many times over in United Methodist churches and Sunday school classes. At a popular level United Methodists have made much of their being a noncreedal denomination. The standard promises currently made by adults on joining the church bear this out. New members are publicly asked to support the church by their prayers, presence, gifts, and service. Not a word is said about holding this or that Christian doctrine. It is, of course, assumed that new members are baptized, and this in turn would suggest that belief in the Trinity is at least implicitly held, but even to frame the matter in this way cuts across the whole ethos of the ritual of the transfer of membership. What the new member may or may not believe simply does not enter into the picture in any serious way. On the contrary, most ministers and members, if asked, would tend to say that the doctrinal hallmark of United Methodism is the freedom it grants to its members to believe as they will. Moreover, this stance, in contrast to, say, that of the Southern Baptists, is seen as a great virtue; it is part of the deep rationale for becoming a United Methodist Christian.

There is no denying the attraction of this posture. Certainly, in the short run, it makes it a lot easier to grow churches. All one has to do to become a member is show up and join on Sunday morning. Moreover, this policy makes life a lot easier for pastors and leaders, for one can set aside the demanding and arduous task of initiating new members into the intellectual content of the Christian faith. Even more pertinent, this way of dealing with membership alleviates the need to ask embarrassing questions about what the new member may or may not believe. In addition, there is no doubt that this fits neatly with a deep impulse which was deliberately adopted by the early Methodists. Thus in the early days of Methodism there was a general policy to eschew any kind of doctrinal test for joining the Methodist Societies. Much thought should be given to this topic, however, before we hastily jump from the practice of early Methodism to the current situation. First, even though there were no doctrinal tests, there were very stiff requirements for joining and remaining in the societies. Second, a clear distinction needs to be made between joining a society and joining a church. It is the latter which is the issue under discussion here. It would be interesting to have a full historical analysis of membership requirements in Methodist denominations over the centuries.

It is not my intention here to dig any deeper into the possible rights and wrongs of this policy. I mention it merely to put on the table one of the crucial questions I want to pursue in this chapter, namely, What does it mean doctrinally to be a United Methodist? Is it correct to say that one can be United Methodist and believe whatever one will? Pressing the issue more sharply, can one be a United Methodist elder or a United Methodist bishop and believe whatever one will? By way of answer to this query I shall proceed, first, by outlining and evaluating the prevailing vision in the church on this issue. Finding this vision profoundly unsatisfactory, I shall attempt, second, to sketch a better alternative and argue for its merits. Then, third, I shall offer rebuttals to several objections which are likely to be made against my proposals.

THE DEEPER VISION BENEATH THE SURFACE

The sketch I have just given of what it is to be a United Methodist is one that is related in a very complex way to what I shall designate as the conventional position on doctrinal matters in the last generation. On the surface the position described has all the hallmarks of doctrinal indifference. It appears to be saying, "It does not matter what you believe; believe anything you like; and you can still be a United Methodist." This is, however, only appearance. What we have here is the popular deposit of a very rich proposal which was hammered out and brought to expression in the sixties and early seventies.

At one level, this proposal did appear to sanction doctrinal indifference. It did indeed appear to say to people that they were free, as United Methodists, to believe whatever they liked. However, at another level, it would be deeply misleading to see the prevailing consensus as sanctioning general doctrinal indifference. On the contrary, the freedom to believe whatever one wanted doctrinally was balanced by a very specific account of what was absolutely required at the level of criterion or norm of belief. One could believe what one wanted precisely because one was required normatively to arrive at one's doctrinal proposals by use of the Methodist quadrilateral. It was commitment to the quadrilateral which made one a United Methodist. In turn, commitment to the quadrilateral held one sharply accountable to what was thought to be the highest possible theological standards, all the while sanctioning radical pluralism at the doctrinal level. In short the quadrilateral did at least three things: first, it set the standard for United Methodist identity; second, it was used comprehensively to foster theological reflection across the face of the church; and, third, it provided the rationale for doctrinal pluralism.

This vision of United Methodist doctrine is so embedded in the life of the church that to question it is nothing short of revolutionary. As I have just indicated, it provides the rationale for the prevailing perception that one can be United Methodist and believe anything. It shows up in editorials in United Methodist newspapers and in agency documents. It comes naturally from the lips of bishops and elders. It has been the staple diet of United Methodist educational literature for a generation and more now. Moreover, it has been central in the examining of candidates for deacons and elders, in that Boards of Ministry have relied heavily upon it in their evaluations. Finally, it is clear that it constitutes the heart of the proposals concerning United Methodist doctrine adopted at the General Conference of 1972. Indeed this in part accounts for its appearance throughout the church. Clearly, any challenge to this whole way of thinking may well prove painful and even alarming to those who have long relied on it.

Yet many in the church have been far from happy. Jerry Walls wrote a penetrating critique of doctrinal pluralism, challenging the very coherence of the notion.[1] The incoherence of pluralism can be articulated in this way. Ecclesial pluralism is the view that all theological or doctrinal positions are to be tolerated within the same ecclesial body. However, one possible and thoroughly tenable theological position is the *ecclesiological* claim that the Christian church is constituted by some particular doctrine, say, the doctrine of the Trinity and that to reject that doctrine, say, in favor of Unitarianism, is to cease to be Christian. Clearly, ecclesial pluralism cannot accommodate this position. Hence its claim to include all theological positions is logically impossible, and it falls prey to incoherence. It is not, therefore, surprising to find that pluralists cannot be consistent in practice. Sooner or later they smuggle in either an ordinary confessional element, like prevenient grace, or an indirect confessional requirement, like the quadrilateral.

More pertinent, Boards of Ministry have been very forthright in insisting on commitment to infant baptism as constitutive of eldership in The United Methodist Church. Characteristically, candidates for ordained ministry are also examined on their commitment to such doctrines as the reality of prevenient grace and justification by faith rather than works. Thus they are evaluated on the basis of very specific doctrines. They are not just accepted or rejected in light of their commitment to the quadrilateral; they are also evaluated in light of material doctrinal norms. What this ambivalence about the doctrinal norms of evaluation shows is that it may well be time to raise some fundamental questions about the prevailing consensus.

WHY WE MUST REJECT THE METHODIST QUADRILATERAL

I want now to propose that this consensus has outlived its usefulness. I shall suggest that the attempt to make the quadrilateral the benchmark of United Methodist identity is unconstitutional, and I shall argue that it is intellectually wrongheaded.

The simplest and deepest objection to be made against the prevailing claims about the quadrilateral and its current status as the ruling doctrinal standard of United Methodism is that it is unconstitutional. As the preparation and debate for the 1988 General Conference makes clear, the only candidates eligible to be the doctrines or doctrinal standards of The United Methodist Church are the *Articles of Religion,* the *Confession of Faith,* Wesley's *Sermons,* and Wesley's *Notes.* We saw in our last chapter the debate, indeed the sharp difference of historical opinion, which lay behind these options. Moreover, we now know how this was resolved. The General Conference of 1988 designated all these documents as the relevant referent for the standards of doctrine covered by the First Restrictive Rule. It is these which constitute our doctrines and doctrinal standards. To ask for anything more or less by way of commitment is profoundly unconstitutional.

To insist on commitment to the quadrilateral is, then, to insist on a norm of identity which goes against the letter and spirit of the First Restrictive Rule. It is to ask members and ministers to hold to a criterion of identity or a standard of doctrine which has nowhere been sanctioned by the appropriate legislative body. Indeed, by the very nature of the case, no additional standard can be imposed on the church, for the First Restrictive Rule makes such revision of the constitution practically impossible.[2] In other words, the quadrilateral could only be used as a doctrinal standard if the relevant enabling legislation to change our doctrinal standards were brought through the General Conference.

It will help at this point if we pause and say a historical word about the quadrilateral. The quadrilateral is a working hypothesis about method in theology, derived from interaction with the Wesley corpus by one of the greatest Methodist scholars of the twentieth century. It was Albert Outler's fascinating attempt to solve tangled questions that crop up in systematic theology in the Western branch of the Christian tradition.

There is no doubting Outler's brilliant contribution to the United Methodist heritage. His work in putting John Wesley on the theological map of the modern world, his splendid provision of a critical edition of Wesley's *Sermons,* his incredibly illuminating comments on both the whole sweep of Wesley's thinking and on its minute nooks and crannies, are an extraordinary gift to the church. I personally owe to Outler my own reappropriation of the Wesleyan tradition at a time in my journey when it had gone entirely dead for me. All future generations of scholars will be indebted to his Herculean labors.

His proposal on the quadrilateral fits naturally into this rich tapestry. As such it deserves our deepest respect and attention. It merits the kind of critical assessment which any theological proposal of this nature deserves. It does not, however, deserve to be treated as an essential element in our constitutional standards of doctrine. Aside from its never having been given this status historically in the constitution, there are at least three very good reasons for this judgment.

First, the current standards of doctrine both in the *Articles of Religion* and in the *Confession of Faith* already provide a substantial treatment of the place of scripture in our doctrinal commitments. To add some kind of statement on the quadrilateral would at best muddy the waters unnecessarily and at worst create theological incoherence. Even if the constitution permitted the possibility, we do not need two sets of materials on scripture, one inside and one outside the existing standards. The material we currently have inside the standards is more than enough for the welfare of the tradition. To add the kind of convoluted proposal which is currently dressed up in the language of the quadrilateral simply makes the church look foolish and doubleminded.

Second, although some sort of vision of the quadrilateral is clearly rooted in aspects of Wesley's *Sermons* and *Notes,* it is precarious in the extreme to argue that it is constitutive of Wesley's theology.[3] What we have is a fruitful hypothesis about Wesley's theology which should be considered alongside other hypotheses in our deliberations. Such historical hypotheses should not be made covert standards of doctrine. This is especially so when, as all informed agreement will attest, it is extremely difficult to argue that Wesley really was a systematic theologian who had worked out intentionally anything as grand as a theological method. In fact this whole way of thinking about Wesley's theological endeavors is inflated and pretentious.

It is easy to fall into the trap of making more of Wesley than he really was and of constructing a grand methodological scheme out of his materials because our current forms of academic socialization tend to lead us to think of doctrinal standards in terms of something akin to the quadrilateral. We instinctively interpret a standard as some kind of grand norm of knowledge or network of norms, given our deep enculturation into Enlightenment forms of rationality. Happily, exposure to the actual nature of our standards can cure us of this restrictive and narrow way of thinking. We need to stand back and take the standards of doctrine that we have, as they are in themselves, rather than impose some predetermined scheme on them. In fact in this field to set up some prior standard for determining the marks of doctrinal standards in advance strikes me as presumptuous and premature. Instead, we should approach the materials already bequeathed to us modestly, with historical awareness, and with sensitivity and creativity.

Third, as it stands the quadrilateral is riddled with problems. It is intrinsically inadequate as a proposal in itself, irrespective of its inadequacy as a summary of theological method in the works of John Wesley. This point is so important that we need to work our way into my reasons for it with some care.

It is surely fair to say that the quadrilateral represents a natural intellectual evolution within the Wesleyan tradition. At its inception the Wesleyan movement was not preoccupied with problems about the warrants for its doctrines. The primary questions faced were: What to teach? How to teach? What to do? As Methodism grew and matured, it was fitting that, as its members became educated, and as it produced its own indigenous thinkers, questions about the grounding for its beliefs would be raised and pursued.

Some Christian traditions take official or canonical actions concerning such proposals. Thus the Roman Catholic Church has given special status to the work of Thomas Aquinas, and in the Eastern Orthodox Church the work of Gregory of Palamas is held in very high regard. Over the centuries the Anglican Church has made much of its commitment to scripture, tradition, and reason. In recent years a whole school of Reformed thinkers has emerged out of the Calvinistic tradition, attempting to develop an account of the warrant for religious beliefs which is in keeping with the Reformed faith as a whole. Perhaps the Methodist quadrilateral represents the first serious attempt to develop a theory of knowledge for the Wesleyan tradition. As such it is work on the frontier of the tradition, which might be seen as somewhat makeshift and hasty, yet invaluable as a first effort in the field.[4] This is a very plausible suggestion.

However, it does nothing to bring the quadrilateral inside the boundaries of the doctrinal standards of The United Methodist Church. The latter is constituted for the most part by material of an entirely different nature and order.

Nor, for that matter, does it settle the crucial question as to whether the quadrilateral is the best way to articulate the insights about religious knowledge which may lie buried in the bosom of the tradition.

My suspicions that it is far from adequate in this regard are prompted by the fact that the whole idea of running together scripture, tradition, reason, and experience is like mixing the proverbial apples and oranges. At its heart the quadrilateral involves a fatal running together of a reduced account of ecclesial canons with the norms of Enlightenment theories of knowledge.[5] To express the matter graphically, it is a hastily contrived shotgun wedding between scripture and tradition, the bride provided by the church, and reason and experience, the bridegroom, provided by the European Enlightenment.[6] As such it involves us in intellectual commitments which are at best debatable and at worst untenable. Over against this our current commitments about the source of our knowledge of God, as found in our current standards of doctrine, are modest and unpretentious. Indeed, it would be altogether accurate to say that we have a brief doctrine of scripture rather than even the contours of a serious theory of knowledge.

In order to press home the crucial difference between the canons of the church and norms of religious knowledge, it is helpful to imagine the following scenario. Suppose United Methodists as a whole were faced with the prospects of martyrdom. Suppose, further, they were given a choice. Half of them were asked to give up their commitment to the incarnation or face death; and half of them were asked to give up the quadrilateral or face death. Does not our automatic response to these alternatives, namely, our immediate recognition that it is the former alone which would constitute Christian martyrdom, indicate that it is bizarre to put the quadrilateral on a level with the actual standards of doctrine currently given to us in the church? Certainly, this is how it appears to this writer.

To put the matter formally, it is wrongheaded to place scripture and tradition in the same category with reason and experience. The latter, for what they are worth, are concepts of justification or rationality. They represent a summary analysis of the kinds of entities which are candidates for winning races in the field of theory of knowledge, a technical field in modern philosophy known as epistemology. Scripture and tradition are nothing of the kind. To put them in the same category with reason and experience will only ensure that the deep intent and purpose of scripture and tradition will be misread and misapplied. To sense the force of this, all one has to do is to imagine how silly it is to construe, say, the book of Revelation or the Gospel according to John as some sort of norm in the theory of knowledge. What applies to a part, applies likewise to the whole. Equally, it is ridiculous to think of the Nicene Creed, a crucial piece of Christian tradition, as a norm of knowledge. Indeed to treat it as such a norm will lead to a false reading of its content and purpose. Hence the quadrilateral harbors within it deeply destructive consequences which its proponents have barely begun to identify, much less resolve.

At another level, it is misleading to think of reason and experience as particularly helpful as solutions to queries in the theory of knowledge. By abstracting from the actual, concrete ways by which we identify and evaluate various kinds of evidence, insight, and argument, they take us into a kind of illusory world of intellectual security which masks the need for far more extensive work in the field.

Worse still, commitment to the quadrilateral weds us to the kind of evidentialism which insists that somehow all our beliefs, if they are to be rationally permitted, have to be worked up by everyone from scratch. Hence it cuts the individual off from the natural world of testimony, tradition, conscience, and the like, which are integral to the life of the mind. In addition, it construes Christian believers as rational, autonomous agents constantly applying a calculus to all their beliefs, all the way from their basic beliefs about the natural order and their ordinary beliefs concerning what they had for breakfast right through to their deepest convictions about the blessed Trinity or the work of Christ. This is a wholly artificial way to think of the formation of one's religious convictions which will only serve to erode systematically the subtle network of one's doctrinal commitments.

An additional problem with the quadrilateral is this. It is practically unworkable. What it suggests is that we should tackle every theological problem by working through all the relevant evidence to be culled from the sources of scripture, tradition, reason, and experience. This is an impossible feat for any finite mind to carry out with any degree of seriousness. In many cases there is potentially a vast array of evidence which would have to be worked through before one could reach any conclusion. In the end probably only God could use it; thankfully God does not need it.

The quadrilateral, even in its most carefully stated form, does not show how we are to resolve potential conflicts between the various sources. It is naive to think that, in a conflict between, say, scripture and reason, scripture will be allowed to carry the day. Equally, in a conflict between, say, tradition and experience, it is difficult to see how tradition will survive if it is seen as in conflict with experience. The history of modern theology shows all too clearly that reason and experience will win every time over against scripture and tradition. The only way to provide a serious case for the primacy of scripture and a potential place for tradition here is to deploy a substantial account of revelation, a term which is not really taken seriously in expositions of the quadrilateral. Hence the attempt to rescue the quadrilateral by asserting the primacy of scripture really comes across as a species of arbitrary dogmatism.

Commitment to the quadrilateral takes us, then, into a murky underworld of minimalist, philosophical speculation which can only be satisfying to those who want to solve deep problems about the nature of rationality, justification, and knowledge by means of tidy and deceptive slogans. It betrays a shallow grasp of the serious problems in epistemology which yet remain to be solved. Even at its best, the quadrilateral is banal and hopelessly simplistic when one examines it in the light of the progress which has been made in this arena in the last generation. To allow this kind of material in any way to interfere with or replace the rich, specific, concrete doctrines of incarnation and grace, of salvation and Trinity, of sin and sacrament, of sanctification and judgment, of creation and atonement, is to offer us stones when we asked for bread. It is small wonder that the church as a whole is doctrinally weak after a generation of such a diet. Perhaps it is a miracle that the church is still alive at all.

Of course, the immediate question all this raises is, What then should we do with the quadrilateral? More generally, what should we do with all the material presented to General Conference on the quadrilateral and other material like that given in the section of the *Discipline* that deals with our theological task? These are important questions which need to be answered. The short answer is this: We should scrap this kind of amateur philosophy for good and all. The church can well do without it. This answer is, of course, too abrupt, so I shall happily return to it later. What needs to be emphasized here, however, is that these questions are completely beside the point of the central question at issue. That question is focused on how we are to identify our canonical standards of doctrine. On this matter the quadrilateral is a complete irrelevance. By appropriate legislation, our standards are clearly constituted by the *Articles of Religion,* the *Confession of Faith,* Wesley's *Sermons,* and Wesley's *Notes.* Even those who might still want to rescue the quadrilateral will have to concede this crucial point. Whether these constitute adequate or even appropriate standards is also beside the point. For better or worse, these are our standards and they cannot now be undone.

A NEW VISION OF OUR IDENTITY

This conclusion has deep implications for the question of how we are to conceive our identity as a church. Once we accept this conclusion, then it is clearly wrong to think of United Methodism as a pluralist church. The construal of the quadrilateral as our doctrinal standard and doctrinal pluralism are simply siamese twins. They come together. Hence it is no surprise that the General Conference of 1988 rejects the language of pluralism and rightly prefers to speak of diversity. If, then, we reject not only the quadrilateral but the pluralism that accompanied it, what alternative description should we use to capture the new developments? Let me cut immediately to the chase and sketch out what seems to me to be the obvious alternative. The only real alternative is for United Methodism to face the fact that it has its own way of being a confessional church. In its constitution from the beginning it has been committed as a church to material standards of doctrine. It has confessed the Christian faith in terms of its *Articles of Religion;* in more recent years, at the merger in 1968 and at the General Conference of 1988, it has additionally identified as its material standards of doctrine the *Confession of Faith,* together with Wesley's *Sermons* and *Notes.* To say this, that is to say that we are a confessional church, is to say no more and no less than what is required of us by the constitution of the church. How might we best spell out this claim? Let me make four main points.

First, it is worth noting at the outset that the switch from the older model of identity to my proposed revision does not constitute a switch from a nonrestrictive to a restrictive model. The commitment to the quadrilateral is profoundly restrictive. It requires one to accept a thoroughly debatable philosophical proposal. It commits one to what we might call an indirect confessional account of our identity. On pain of not being United Methodist, we are required to adhere to a particular theological method. This is thoroughly restrictive and exclusive in its own way. As a philosopher, I would have to cease to be a United Methodist, if I were to hold that it was essential to the United Methodist tradition.

Second, on the revised account it is surely the case that we are indeed a confessional church. Unlike, say, the Unitarians and Southern Baptists, we are committed to a body of specific doctrine which is spelled out clearly in a series of doctrinal propositions. This is patently visible in our *Articles of Religion* and in our *Confession of Faith*. Given this, it is misleading to claim that we are a noncreedal church. Such a claim is generally taken to mean that we do not have a body of doctrine to which we are committed. Technically, of course, we do not have a creed, like, say, the Apostles' Creed or the Nicene Creed.[7] It is the move from this claim to the more radical claim that we do not have a body of standard doctrine which is completely unwarranted. The *Articles of Religion* and the *Confession of Faith* prove exactly the opposite. To test this claim concretely all we have to do is ask, Is The United Methodist Church committed, say, to the doctrine of the Trinity, or to the doctrine of justification by grace through faith? Surely the only viable answer is an affirmative one. Once we grant this, the claim that United Methodism is a confessional church is immediately secured.

Third, the actual content of our standards puts its primary emphasis on a delicate balance between what we have absorbed from the church down through the centuries and what we ourselves have developed in our rich encounter with the gospel. Here we must be very careful not to be put off by the rather archaic way in which our doctrines were originally expressed. To modern ears and eyes, articles of religion and confessions of faith are not exactly as common as, say, a short political manifesto or a carefully constructed seminary credo. However, it is parochial and ahistorical to expect anything other than a set of articles and a confession of faith from a church which has deep roots in the Protestant tradition. *The crucial point to be made is that the primary content of the doctrinal standards is Christian doctrine.* Moreover, that doctrine is not some sectarian or partisan rendering of the faith. We take our stand resolutely within the faith of the church universal, confessing the common faith of the church down through the ages. Hence we confess the great doctrines of Trinity, original sin, incarnation, atonement, justification by faith, the last judgment, and the like. Then, within that, we insist on our own distinctive doctrines of prevenient grace, assurance, sanctification, the catholic spirit, and the like.

We can also see, by the way, exactly why it is so wrong to construe United Methodism as a Fundamentalist denomination in any way, shape, or form. We identify ourselves not as a narrow sect, holding a reduced set of doctrines, but as a church which stands in the historical Christian tradition, holding to the great verities of the faith confessed by the teachers of the patristic church and embracing some of the central doctrines recovered at the Protestant Reformation. Moreover, we clearly are not committed to even an echo of the Fundamentalist doctrine of scripture, as the relevant articles of the *Discipline* make clear. We are not even committed to Wesley's own confused and misleading comments on the inspiration of scripture.

Fourth, it is clear that United Methodism intends both to say that its doctrines are scripturally grounded and that the scriptures themselves must be seen in doctrinal categories. Consider the following carefully crafted article on scripture.

> We believe the Holy Bible, Old and New Testaments, reveals the Word of God so far as it is necessary for our salvation. It is to be received through the Holy Spirit as the true rule and guide for faith and practice. Whatever is not revealed in or established by the Holy Scriptures is not to be made an article of faith nor is it to be taught as essential to salvation.

This is Article IV of the *Confession of Faith*. Here is Article V of the *Articles of Religion*.

> The Holy Scripture containeth all things necessary to salvation; so that whatsoever is not read therein, nor may be proved thereby, is not to be required of any man that it should be believed as an article of faith, or be thought requisite or necessary to salvation. In the name of the Holy Scripture we do understand those canonical books of the Old and New Testaments of whose authority was never any doubt in the Church. The names of the canonical books are: . . .

Two things should be noted here. First, the articles on scripture are not positioned at the beginning. They crop up after the material on the Trinity, on Jesus Christ, and on the Holy Spirit. I suspect that this displays an entirely proper trinitarian and theocentric focus for our doctrine as a whole. Second, the articles are very modest in what they say about scripture. They insist on the soteriological purpose of scripture in bringing us to salvation, and they systematically rule out the appeal to any other source as the norm of Christian doctrine. In other words, they make it clear that United Methodism is at heart a scriptural church which looks to the Holy Bible, as it phrases it, as its authority in doctrinal matters. As such this leaves a host of matters to be explored and filled in. This is as far as it gets in the matter of theological methodology. In fact, it strikes me as exaggerated and misdirected to try to construct some kind of theological methodology out of our standards of doctrine.

RESPONSE TO OBJECTIONS

Before moving to the healing significance of United Methodist doctrine, it is worth pausing to deal briefly with a network of objections to this shift of perspective.

Objection one: Does not the fact that the standards are made of a variety of materials show that it is wrong to see United Methodism as a confessional church? Does not a confessional church, by definition, have a single confession rather than the accumulation of material gathered together in the current standards?

Reply: The claim that a truly confessional church can have only one confession is thoroughly artificial. A church can confess its faith in a variety of materials. Indeed in the United Methodist case, the *Articles of Religion* and the *Confession of Faith* are remarkably similar in content; the duplication is a kind of historical accident which is bequeathed by the contingencies of history. Moreover, there is ample precedent in the Anglican tradition in the use of sermons as possible standards of doctrine.

Objection two: Is not the content of the standards simply a dated eighteenth-century rendering of the Christian faith foisted on us by early Methodists?

Reply: This totally ignores the extent to which the content of the standards was chosen not because of their recent appearance but because they captured the heart of the faith as it developed over the centuries. To reject this material is not just to reject the faith of the early Methodists, it is to set aside the living heritage of the Christian tradition over the centuries. It is to leap from the early church into our own day without going through the historical, intellectual developments of the church through time.

Objection three: Does not this analysis suggest that it is possible to draw a kind of boundary between those who are in and those who are out, and is this not only a deep departure from the Methodist heritage but also something intrinsically wrong in itself?

Reply: Certainly, this analysis suggests that there are boundaries between those who are in and those who are out. The fact that The United Methodist Church has clear procedures for trial shows that there is nothing odd in this. The existence of such procedures only supports the reading of the tradition suggested here.

Moreover, there is nothing wrong about having boundaries. Suppose an elder decides that the Salvation Army was right to give up the practice of Holy Communion and, believing that The United Methodist Church should follow suit, he quietly drops such services from the liturgy? Or suppose an elder comes to the conclusion that certain racial groups are not fully human and, therefore, are not included in the salvation brought by Christ, and she begins to teach this systematically in her local congregation? Or suppose an elder begins to teach that salvation is not by grace but by works? Or suppose he insists in season and out that speaking in tongues is essential to a full Christian experience of God? In such cases it would be strange for The United Methodist Church simply to say that these teachings should be tolerated, as if it had no right or responsibility to draw boundaries and ask its elders to abide by them. Indeed, the refusal to draw boundaries is a moral failure in such circumstances rather than a virtue. Refusal displays the romantic illusion that somehow hard decisions about the content of the tradition can be avoided.

Objection four: Does not this entail that we shall have to face the possibility of heresy trials?

Reply: Of course, it does. The possibility of recourse to heresy trials has always been there, as the provision for them in the *Discipline* makes evident.

Nor should this at all worry us, as if suddenly the church were about to fall from grace. There is no good moral or spiritual reason why United Methodism, like any other self-respecting body, should not take action in order to prevent its good offices from being used for the propagation of doctrines that undermine its identity and witness. Moreover, we can trust United Methodists to find their own way to relearn how best to apply suitable measures for doctrinal discipline. To approach this whole matter in a spirit of fear and suspicion is a clear sign of insecurity and immaturity. There are ample safeguards already in place to ward off unfairness and malice.

Objection five: But does not our Lord call us only to two fundamental commitments, namely, to love God and love our neighbor as ourselves? So is not the heart of the faith a matter of religious life, rather than an insistence on some kind of uniformity of religious belief?

Reply: The mistake here is to play life off against belief, or moral commitment off against doctrine, as if somehow we have to choose between the two. United Methodism is not simply a kind of moral social club which is bereft of doctrinal underpinnings. It is committed to loving God and loving one's neighbor in the context of a rich intellectual heritage which identifies that God in trinitarian terms, and which spells out a classical understanding of how that God has made true love possible through his sacrificial incarnation in the world and through his precious sending of the Holy Spirit. To cut away the latter and turn the tradition into a pious humanitarian sect without sacraments and without doctrinal identity is to do violence to the tradition at its foundations.

Objection six: Did not John Wesley have only one condition for membership in the Methodist Societies, namely, the desire to flee from the wrath to come? Are you not then abandoning the core of the Methodist understanding of membership in the church?

Reply: the question assumes that United Methodism is still simply a movement in the Anglican tradition of the eighteenth century. This is plainly false. For better or worse United Methodism is now a worldwide Christian denomination which became a church more than two centuries ago. Hence it cannot avoid facing up to its own identity as a church. The societies are gone, and we must come to terms with our existence as a Christian communion complete with appropriate polity and doctrine.

Objection seven: Do not churches that hold to doctrinal commitment tend to be narrow and restrictive, something which is precisely the opposite of Methodist sensibilities? Should we not focus on personal commitment to God rather than on doctrine?

Reply: The question as it stands harbors an internal inconsistency. In addition, it begs the question about the nature of United Methodist sensibilities.

The internal inconsistency lies in its appeal for commitment of a very general sort, while rejecting the need for doctrinal commitment. One does not commit to Christ in a vacuum. There will always be some kind of doctrinal core involved. Moreover, any call for commitment will set boundaries. Whether those boundaries will be narrow or restrictive has to be judged on merit in each case. Generalities that trade on spatial images of narrowness are useless and misleading at this juncture until we can spell out what exactly the boundaries are. As I have already argued, there is nothing narrow about commitment to the shared, ecumenical faith of the church or the distinctives of the Wesleyan tradition. If someone thinks these are narrow and restrictive compared with other traditions, then let the case be argued in detail. In the absence of such a case, we do not really have a charge to answer. On the other side, the current requirement of commitment to the Methodist quadrilateral is extremely exclusive in its effects.

Furthermore, to claim that somehow United Methodism is not committed to a specific doctrinal identity is to invoke the very claim which has been systematically dismantled over the last two chapters. Mere repetition of that claim will no longer carry the day; there will have to be new, substantial arguments mounted to support the deeply flawed consensus of the last generation. In addition, it is plainly naive to think that one can have commitment without getting into doctrinal commitments. Again we are playing off alternatives, in this case, commitment against doctrine, which really belong naturally together as a single whole.

Objection eight: All this is well and good, but is it not too late in the day to call The United Methodist Church to fidelity to its own doctrinal identity?

Reply: This is a good question, but it is beside the point of this chapter. The question masks an understandable attempt to predict future developments in United Methodism, which are out of range of the present argument. How things develop may well depend on what we do with the practical implications of this proposal and how far we are prepared to work for deep renewal of the faith in our midst. To this latter topic we now turn.

Chapter Four

Doctrinal Healing and the Renewal of the Church

THREE CHEERS FOR RENEWAL

One of the more heartening features of life within The United Methodist Church today is the massive quest for renewal which surfaces in different forms in various places. There has been a flood of literature directed at offering a diagnosis of what has gone wrong and how to put things right. One can easily become overwhelmed with the various proposals on offer. Taken as a whole, however, they display a lively debate, which is a sign of the vitality of the tradition. Dead traditions do not argue about how to find a way into the future; they simply give up hope and fall prey to cynicism. Also encouraging is the way a host of people are seeking to invent new delivery systems for the content of the classical means of grace. The Holy Spirit is re-equipping the church with numerous new ways of encountering the gospel and making progress in the faith.

It is seldom, however, that we have explored the extent to which renewal is dependent on healing the doctrinal amnesia we have sought to cure by recovering a more adequate historical memory. Doctrine is still seen as harmful and divisive or as a curb on freedom and creativity. This is a strange judgment, for in the healing of the church we cannot avoid making doctrinal decisions. In this chapter I want to argue a case for the place of doctrine in the renewal of mission, spirituality, and faith. The time is long since past when we can pretend that basic Christian teaching is irrelevant to continued growth in grace and faith.

I shall begin by making some preliminary, stage-setting remarks on the topic of church renewal, drawing attention to the breakdown of the traditional Protestant language for renewal over the last century or so. Then, I want to look at the state of the church by identifying some specific problems which need to be tackled. Third, I want to go beyond these problems and identify a wider horizon in which they must be located. Not surprisingly, I shall suggest that many of the problems we face are intimately related to doctrinal amnesia and neglect. This will pave the way for the fourth and final section where I shall briefly indicate the relation between doctrinal renewal and the wider renewal we seek.

THE SECOND GREAT AWAKENING IS OVER

One of the most striking features of today's debate about the renewal of the church is that the traditional way of conceiving renewal has collapsed over the last century. The classical language for renewal in North American Protestantism was captured most basically in the concepts of revival and awakening. These terms were so intrinsic to the very history of North American culture that some years ago William G. McLoughlin offered a fascinating overview of the history of the United States of America by arguing that the nation as a whole could be seen as moving through no fewer than four awakenings or revivals.[1] McLoughlin's illuminating failure to sustain his analysis when he applied it to the developments of the 1960s displays, in my judgment, the collapse of these concepts in the last half of the twentieth century. The last great awakening, according to McLoughlin, was the "God is dead" movement of the 1960s. Anyone remotely aware of the meaning of "awakenings" in the

75

eighteenth century will recognize immediately that the classical concept has simply disintegrated in his analysis.

The classical concepts of awakening and revival in the eighteenth century are themselves of great interest. The ambiguities buried within them point in part to the internal reasons for their demise. An awakening or revival originally meant something quite specific in the life of the church. Broadly conceived, they were terms used to describe a widespread work of the Holy Spirit in which nominal Christians or church members were so awakened or revived by the power of the Holy Spirit that they were converted to a living faith and became active members of the church. In the First Great Awakening thousands upon thousands were swept into the kingdom through the preaching and labors of figures like Jonathan Edwards, George Whitefield, and John Wesley. In the Second Great Awakening a similar story can be told with respect to the work of its great architect and theorist, Charles G. Finney.

From the beginning, however, the concepts of awakening and revival were profoundly unstable. Many Christians in the classical Protestant tradition found the whole idea of revival or awakening distasteful. In the case of both Great Awakenings, there was a vast body of polemical literature which made manifest the controversies that swirled in and around them. For our purposes it is sufficient to draw attention to two crucial observations.

First, for many the First Great Awakening was bound up with millennial and nationalist aspirations which were dubious in the extreme. Thus Jonathan Edwards saw in the events of his day a fulfillment of a prophetic hope that there would be a great and glorious work of the Lord which would far surpass what happened in the outpouring of the Spirit at Pentecost, and he argued that the New World was the chosen geographical location for this new and special work of God.[2] Both these convictions have lingered on in the Protestant underworld and in the nether regions of North

American political and cultural life. They should not be confused with the descriptive claim, that, like it or not, the United States of America is the modern empire. Thus the United States of America has enormous influence on other cultures and nations. For this reason the renewal of the Christian tradition in the United States is of more than parochial significance.

Second, Charles Finney changed the face of revival forever when he argued with great enthusiasm and verbal skill that revivals were fundamentally something that human beings could bring about by their pious and religious acts. What was originally a *surprising* work of God in which the heart was *strangely* warmed became a routine and mechanized series of events within the life of the church. Revivals became something humans organized and engineered at will. This radically changed the whole ethos of the concept of revival, so much so that it is now represented by a series of meetings in the annual life of the church, which, if they are held at all, are seen as a kind of motivational rally. Such a conception is very different from the older conception, which lingers on in the Celtic fringes of Britain.

These developments themselves have fueled the collapse of the old language. The original concepts of awakening and revival live on in nooks and crannies of the modern church, and they surface from time to time in Christian television, but they are now effectively dead in the life of the church. They are tied to populist aspirations which have been eroded by secularization, they are associated with premodern conceptions of theology, and they fail to kindle today's Christian imagination on a grand scale.

THE SEARCH FOR RENEWAL

The notions of awakening and revival have effectively been replaced by the concept of renewal. Along with such terms as "restoration," "retrieval," and "revitalization," "renewal" has become a new, safe, code word for revival. Proposals on how to pin down this rather fuzzy notion are now legion.

In the last thirty years we have had a number of movements purposely dedicated to various kinds of renewal. We have had in turn the renewal of biblical theology, liturgical renewal, lay witness renewal, and above all, charismatic renewal. Within the last ten years or so there has been a flurry of literature attempting to offer a variety of proposals for the renewal of the church. Many of these have been sociological in orientation, taking as their cue the numerical decline of the mainline Christian churches.[3] In response to these proposals church leaders have been quick to adopt various schemes of church growth as the way out of our current malaise; so much so, that evangelism has been effectively reduced to church growth by most Protestant denominations. In more recent times there has been a shift to thinking of renewal in explicitly doctrinal terms, but it would be premature to claim that this shift is either substantial or likely to be sustained.

The great diversity of proposals available in this latter arena is worth noting. They range all the way from an appeal to return to the particular roots of the mainline denominations, represented by John Leith, to a vast repudiation of the classical Christian tradition and its replacement by certain chosen elements of Pagan and Enlightenment ideology, represented by Rosemary Ruether. In and around these there are proposals to get the church to adopt a whole new epistemological strategy, as argued at length by Lesslie Newbigin in England; to retrieve a thoroughly fundamentalist doctrine of scripture, as stated by James Draper among the Southern Baptists; to recover the multifaceted gifts of the Holy Spirit, as articulated by Cardinal Suenens; or to encounter anew and afresh the life-giving mysteries of the

Eucharist, as forcefully articulated by Alexander Schmemann. In other cases the call to renewal involves the invita-
tion to recover the ecumenical consensus of the church, as
seen most conspicuously in the recent writings of Thomas
Oden. Alternatively, it may involve the critical, postmodern
reappropriation of the legacy of the great Augustine, as
densely argued and presented by the English lay theologian,
John Milbank. The latter proposals take us into very deep
waters indeed. They fit very naturally with the massive
interpretations of our intellectual ills, which have recently
been developed by figures like Basil Mitchell, Alasdair
MacIntyre, and Charles Taylor.[4]

The conclusions to be drawn from this brief overview of
the state of the question can be accurately summarized in
three closely related claims.

First, in the West, Christians as a whole are currently
undergoing a profound process of soul-searching. Old
coalitions are breaking down; new coalitions are forming.
Christians have been driven both by the decline of their
numbers and by changes in the culture to examine in new
ways the state of the church and the faith. In doing so they
have been forced to invent a new vocabulary of renewal to
capture the dynamics of debate.

Second, it is clear from the variety of proposals now
offered that Christians are divided both with respect to the
diagnosis of our ills and with respect to the prescriptions for
our cure. These divisions run very deep indeed. They cut to
the very heart of Christian identity in the contemporary
world. They engage us in debates concerning our continuity
with the church of the ages and about our relations to the
cultural, intellectual, and political trends that have constituted the driving forces of the modern era.[5] Claims and
counterclaims in this arena are contested from top to bot-
tom.

Third, judgments in this domain are inescapably doctrinal in character. What is at stake is nothing less than the remaking of the church, so no account of diagnosis or prescription can be given without deploying concepts which are doctrinal in nature. We will be driven to think in terms which relate to such matters as the content of the gospel, the nature of our existence as creatures and sinners, the character of salvation, and the marks of the church. This is not to say that sociological, philosophical, and other categories may not be needed; nor is it to say that our prescriptions may not be practical in the extreme. We are simply facing the fact that ecclesial renewal, as interpreted by serious Christians, is ultimately constituted by the work of God in the healing and saving of our fractured existence.

It has already become clear that proposals about renewal involve some sort of diagnosis of what has gone wrong in the life of the church. We can immediately imagine a catalog of possibilities. Things can go wrong for a whole host of reasons. Thus the church can become captive to ignorance, moral corruption, spiritual apathy, organizational dysfunction, heresy, apostasy, intellectual confusion, loss of memory, loss of identity, internal schism, failure of nerve—the list is endless. There is, then, no *one* way that the church can go wrong; sin is so manifold that it can break out in many directions all at once. I sometimes wonder whether different cultural and national groups or various Christian denominations sin differently. As one witty observer once pointed out to me, "The problem with the English is that they are moral, but it is extremely difficult to make them religious. The problem with the Irish is that they are religious, but it is virtually impossible to make them moral." The lesson to be drawn from this is clear. We can only begin to think through what we mean by renewal when we have specified relatively substantially our problems and what lies beneath them or below them. This is a precarious enterprise but let me launch forth nevertheless.

A CATALOG OF CONCERNS

Over the last several years, as I have traveled in church work I have been asking people to identify the central problems, as they see them, in the church as a whole. Adding my own observations and reflections, I discern the following ten items as sources of anxiety. The order is given more or less at random.

1. The first problem on everyone's mind is the continuing decline in membership. This is typically interpreted by observers as simply a crass concern with numbers. This is much too facile an analysis. In my judgment people naturally begin with numbers because this is an objective kind of yardstick which everyone can readily understand. Moreover, it permits us to begin identifying our problems in ways that are minimally threatening, for in speaking of numbers we initially avoid taking any kind of theological risk.

2. A second problem which is not far behind the decline in numbers is concern with apportionments or monies sent to the central bureaucracies. Often this is seen as a kind of church tax which keeps increasing, as if it were out of control. As in the first case this should not be seen in crassly material terms. D. L. Moody used to say that people were not truly converted until salvation reached down into their pockets and wallets. Money is never a purely secular affair from a Christian point of view. What people are worried about is that the decline in revenues coupled with the increase in apportionments to central funds signifies a deeper spiritual malaise in the church. It shows a lack of trust on many levels. For those who give less, it reveals a lack of trust in the current values of the church as a whole; for the

members who do give their money to the church, it shows a lack of trust in its central organizations.

3. This leads very naturally into a third source of anxiety. Many in the church are deeply alienated from the central agencies of the church. On this score dissatisfaction is rampant. Some leading pastors would immediately cut off the funding to certain central agencies, if they had the power to do so. Their primary complaint is a lack of accountability among agencies to the grass roots of the church. Agency leaders and workers are perceived as sovereign unto themselves, able to pull the relevant political strings to further their favored agendas.

4. A fourth nest of problems is constituted by worries about the current leadership of the church. On this score the sense is that most designated leaders, such as bishops and superintendents, lack either the knowledge, the fortitude, the skill, or the will to bring about renewal in the church as a whole. Hedged around by committees, overwhelmed by extensive burdens, holding political debts and dues of some sort, perhaps unsure of the boundaries of their power and authority, most leaders have little time left to devote to thinking through the renewal of the church. Those who do scarcely know where to begin. In these circumstances many clergy and laity are like scattered sheep, inclined to turn to any charismatic leader or group who offers to lead them to the promised land. Consequently the church divides into parties and movements which may prove invaluable in sustaining a vision and energy, but which also break the fragile bonds of unity and fellowship in the body as a whole.

5. A fifth area of anxiety is the seminaries. The main concern here is that seminaries are perceived, at heart, as being out of touch with the church. Often this perception is very vague and unsubstantiated, for most lay people do not have much of a clue about seminary life. Their sense is that

seminaries fail to nurture seminarians in a deep way in the gospel and the faith of the church; they fail to provide a proper balance between intellectual reflection or formation and the practice of ministry; and they often reflect doctrinal convictions and values which are incompatible with the convictions of the church.

6. A sixth concern is the general moral and doctrinal hollowness of the church in its preaching and teaching. At one level one never knows what will appear in the sermon on Sunday morning. There is little of substance to nourish the soul in sanctification or in the fight against temptation and evil. More often than not, one is offered a mixture of thin doctrinal pabulum and moralistic platitude. Overall the impression is given that the preacher's task is to act as a minor chaplain to a culture which expects to be soothed and massaged on a regular basis. The deeply distinctive content of the faith may not be set aside completely, but it is frequently found to be accommodated to the changing whims of the culture.

7. This is counterbalanced by a seventh concern, represented by the encroachment of a radical agenda into the institutions and fabric of the church. On the surface the goal of this agenda is to make the church more inclusive. The aim is to make the church more open, for example, to minorities and women, so that the church can make full use of all the gifts and talents bestowed upon us in creation and redemption. This agenda is one that most mainline Christians are entirely happy to embrace. It is difficult to find United Methodists who are opposed to the full participation of all in the life of the church. However, in an ironic twist of fortune, this agenda can readily be translated into a radical theological and political agenda that ends up excluding or ostracizing those who hold to the classical trinitarian faith of the church. The result is considerable alienation and frustration among those who sense that this constitutive

component of Christian identity is deeply compromised. Furthermore, this agenda can create an atmosphere where the bonds of fellowship in Christ are broken by a division of the church into a host of rival parties and caucuses. In addition, it fosters a climate of intimidation, silence, fear, and indoctrination, which its creators generally fail to perceive.

8. Lurking in the neighborhood is a related and even deeper concern, namely the fear that sooner or later United Methodism will be convulsed by institutional division. The likely cause and occasion for this is some kind of climactic disagreement over the propriety of homosexual behavior. Underneath and around this issue are sharp conflicts about the nature of authority and the norms of Christian identity. It is a serious mistake to see homosexuality as an isolated issue. Modern obsessions with sex as a subject of debate can easily obscure the deeper questions at stake. At present many mainline denominations are in fact in a state of internal institutional division. Various groups within the church have developed their own network of institutions, mission agencies, leaders, theologies, and ecclesial practices. What prevents explicit division are such factors as pension funds, laws governing the ownership of property, and nostalgia. How long these legal threads can hold a community together is a matter for extensive speculation behind the scenes. Some are far from sure that the civil courts would support the conventional wisdom about the ownership of property and institutions.

9. In one way or another these earlier concerns spill over into worries about the mission of the church. Everyone will agree that adjustments were necessary concerning the missionary work of the church. Changes in world culture, the coming of age of the newer branches of the church on the mission fields, and new questions about interfaith dialogue had to be assimilated. Yet the sense in many quarters is that mission is now mostly reduced to social, political, and humanitarian activity. Where, then, many ask, is the place of

individual conversion to Christ and the planting of new congregations in the current mission of the church across the world? The ambivalence evoked by this question causes pain in many quarters.

10. Finally, there is one more anxiety which many sense lies at the heart of the troubles of the modern church, namely the simple fear that the church has lost its way spiritually. The church, it is believed, is not centered on God; it is not rooted and anchored in the life, death, and resurrection of Jesus Christ; it does not live by the power of the Holy Spirit. Over and against these great articles of the faith, the church is driven by cultural concerns; it centers on various programs rather than on a ministry which deals explicitly and directly with the human hunger for the divine; it lives essentially by self-maintenance rather than by the love of God, by the grace of our Lord Jesus Christ, and by the power of the Holy Spirit. In short the church as a corporate entity has wandered once more off its appointed course.

These are essentially the concerns that I have noted in various conversations with informed lay people in the church. They are echoed by many pastors and leaders. They do not under any circumstances amount to a serious scientific or empirical study of the problems of the modern church. They are based on essentially anecdotal and impressionistic evidence. Moreover, they are merely human assessments; they do not begin to tell us how the Judge of all the earth weighs up the current state of the church. Yet they are important because they name the current view of the church held by many devoted Christians, and at this level of caution and modesty they deserve to be taken seriously.

VICTIMS OF OUR OWN EVANGELISTIC SUCCESS

I now want to push our analysis a little more deeply. Let us take this catalog of woes at face value and ask if we can discern any underlying causes which might somehow be related to many of these problems. Can we find a wider analysis that makes intelligible this depiction of our situation? Eventually I shall get around to the connection with doctrinal amnesia but we must not rush ahead of ourselves. We need to put our current concerns into clear historical perspective. I want to venture the following suggestion: Most of our current problems in United Methodism stem from our initial success in the evangelization of the United States. Expressed pointedly, the church has become the victim of its own missional success. Triumph in evangelism has led to a false security in the area of doctrine, leading to deep amnesia concerning the intellectual content of the faith. Let me explain.

As the history of revival and awakening has made clear, the Christian gospel in America made the advances that it did because the gospel was seen as providing access to the life of the riches of the Triune God revealed in the incarnation of Jesus Christ and made real through the working of the Holy Spirit in the scriptures, in the sacramental life of the church, and in the means of grace. Christianity, on the reading of its nature, was nothing if it was not personal. It involved deep repentance from sin, personal conversion, immersion in the life of the Holy Spirit, the total transformation of the whole of life and culture, and the continuous renewal of the church through the study of scripture, through prayer, through fellowship meetings, and through theological education on a grand scale.

Within this perspective the Christian gospel had its own integrity and autonomy. It was, of course, taken for granted that the Christian faith was true, so massive efforts were made to provide the kind of apologetic and intellectual bulwarks which would convince the skeptic and unbeliever that the Christian faith at its core was worthy of assent. However, the center of gravity was ultimately theocentric.

The core of the matter was located not in argument or intellect but in encounter with the living God. Christianity brought one into encounter with a compassionate God who alone was worthy of worship, homage, and obedience. From this base evangelists, teachers, itinerant preachers, prophets, social reformers, church planters, catechists, prayer warriors, frontier missionaries, educational pioneers, and the like, took off to build a new world and populate it with enthusiastic Christians. The experiment was so successful that there are still folk alive in Texas who were brought up believing that every American was a Christian and have been shocked to discover otherwise.

Success also meant that American Christians created a unique kind of culture. From the enormous reservoir of convictions, themes, and impulses which they found in Christianity, they chose this or that element of the tradition, invented whatever else they felt they needed, and proceeded on course with speed. The positive consequences of this spirit are visible in all sorts of ways. One can see them in the extraordinary vitality of Christians in America, in their brashness and confidence to go out and win the world for Christ, in their optimism, in the simplicity of their reliance upon God, in their tendency to act first and explain later, in their enduring love of small groups and Sunday school classes, in their willingness to engage in instant doctrinal revision, in their readiness to give their money to religious and philanthropic causes, and in their penchant for trying one experiment after another in the pursuit of their religious goals and aspirations.

There is, however, a high price to be paid for this practical and doctrinal inventiveness. Indeed that price too is conspicuously visible. The price can be seen in the tragic history of slavery, racism, and religious exclusion, where crucial components of the Christian moral and doctrinal tradition were set aside at will, or worse still, manipulated to suit economic and self-serving ends. It is also all too visible in the tendency to adopt one fad and ideology after another as the way to the promised land, in the naive optimism about human nature which lies below the surface, in the corruption and heresy which has surfaced in television evangelism, and in the hollowness which stems from a failure to grapple with the full wealth of Christian conviction, piety, and tradition. One crucial consequence of this inventiveness is deeply relevant to any future renewal of the church, namely, the emergence and hearty embrace of what has been aptly called the third schism in the church.[6]

A careful word of explanation is in order here, because American Christians are inventive beyond compare when it comes to movements, denominations, and schisms in the body of Christ. It might be thought then that I am merely speaking of the standard kind of divisiveness which is all too familiar. My central point, however, is a different one. As is well known, the Christian tradition has been fractured at two crucial moments in its history. It broke in two in 1054 with the division between East and West; and then, in the early sixteenth century, within the West, it broke again into Roman Catholicism and the various branches of magisterial Protestantism. As we come to the end of the second millennium, these divisions, however, are minor compared with the really deep division which has rocked the Protestant tradition in the modern period, namely, the division between those who want to jettison the classical faith of the church as expressed in the early creeds and those who do not. The really crucial watershed is how we shall come to terms with this division. The dilemma which has again and again surfaced for us in Protestantism is this: Shall we revise the rich canonical life of the church, say, in its scriptures and creeds, in order to make it credible with its cultural despisers? Or shall we find ways to convert the cultural despisers to a living, personal faith which is rooted in deep intellectual continuity with the faith once for all delivered to the saints? Inability to reach consensus on this issue is one of the fundamental sources of our current troubles. The ultimate issue in the end is doctrinal. Christians are at odds on how to articulate their primary doctrines in the modern world.

Seen from this perspective, one of the root problems, if not the root problem, is the doctrinal confusion and chaos, which have been fueled by massive efforts to make the Christian faith credible in the face of constantly changing philosophical and cultural norms. This lies behind the alienation from the central agencies, the worries about the current leadership, the anxiety about the seminaries, the moral and doctrinal fuzziness of church teaching, the encroachment of radical agendas into the fabric of the church, the fear of institutional division, lack of coherence and will in mission, and the absence of spiritual seriousness and depth. The crucial issue underlying this catalog is one of doctrinal vision. The church is lacking in corporate doctrinal and spiritual focus. It is internally divided about its own identity in the modern world. It is torn between holding to and expressing the classical faith of the church, on the one side, and constantly revising, accommodating, and adjusting that faith to the changing demands and norms of modern culture, on the other. I suspect that this also lies behind the problem of numbers and financial resources. After all, few people are willing to invest their time or their money in an institution which is unfocused and undisciplined in its commitments and convictions.

Perhaps another way to make my central point is to say that we are now having to grapple with the internal secularization of the church itself. Where God and the classical means of grace, such as the teaching of scripture and the great creeds of the church, were systematically eliminated from the public order, they are now being challenged within the church itself. Two developments precipitate this evolution: first, the secularization of the culture, in which Christian teaching and practice is intentionally dismantled in the public order so as to make room for a thoroughly pluralist society, and second, a decision within the church to let the culture set the agenda and norms of the church. In these circumstances the church becomes the mirror image of the culture. It loses its grounding and resourcing in divine revelation as mediated in the great canonical traditions of the church. The moral and intellectual pluralism which is entirely appropriate in a post-Christian society is now hailed as obligatory in the church itself.

THE NEED FOR A FRESH IMMERSION IN THE FAITH

What then is to be done? It is obvious that there is no easy way out of our current predicament. Part of our predicament is that we are in deep disagreement as to how to describe our situation. If, however, the analysis I have just given is near to the truth, then there can be no doubt as to what has to be done. In terms of logical priority, the first item of business must surely be the massive retrieval of the great canonical traditions of the church. The church as a whole needs to immerse itself in the gospel, in the scriptures, in the sacraments, in the classical disciplines of the Christian life, and above all, in the great classical doctrines of the church as represented by the early fathers and the creeds.

It is important not to confuse this proposal with some kind of simpleminded, traditional conservatism. Immersion in the tradition brings with it startling surprises for everyone. Deep immersion is likely to be very radical in its consequences. The crucial difference to register is this. Traditionalists and renewalists both look positively to tradition. The former expects *confirmation* of the status quo; the latter looks for the *healing* of the status quo. The former already knows the outcome; the latter is on the alert for the strange new surprises which lie hidden in the womb of the church, as the church awaits the working of the Holy Spirit.

Moreover, this proposal can be taken up as readily by the doubting Thomas among us as it can be by the faithful Mary. Surprising as it may seem, one does not need to believe in advance. In fact, our beliefs are not under the control of our will. All that is required is the decision to embark on a patient and serious search which in faith will accept that the tradition is a treasure to be explored. This in fact is how renewal came, for example, with Luther and Wesley. They took to immersion in the scriptures, to study of the tradition, to intentional participation in the sacramental life of the church, to prayer, and to extended conversation with their friends. It was precisely because they did not know in themselves how to proceed that they took this line. It was only as they proceeded in this faith that they rediscovered the doctrinal treasures of the church.

To be sure, these treasures will be reappropriated in our own times in our own way, so we are not at all ignoring the fact that every generation has its own voice and has its own contribution to make to the doctrinal legacy of the church. What is being stressed is that deep doctrinal retrieval is absolutely pivotal for the healing of the church.

This will not be easy, for we do not mean by this some simple microwave solution to our problems, as if we could reach into the freezer and pick up the good old-time religion and serve it up after instant heating in the nearest oven. The *reception* of the canonical traditions of the church is as important as their content. Unfortunately, the reception of this material has been destroyed for many by our Enlightenment sensibilities. For the great teachers of the church, knowledge of God was only possible when we approach God in humility. For many Enlightenment figures, such "monkish" virtues were laughed out of court. The canonical traditions are gifts of the Holy Spirit given to us for our salvation and healing. They are therefore to be

91

received in a spirit of repentance and humility, of struggle and hope, of faith and godly fear. This spirit too is a gift of the Holy Spirit, characteristically mediated to us in the fellowship of the church, as we are led by God on a journey of moral renovation and holiness. That moral renovation is made possible through the death and resurrection of Jesus Christ, the Son of God, and its ultimate fulfillment is so to share in the mind and life of Christ that we become nothing less than sons and daughters of the living God. In the end the renewal of the church involves this simple but manifold immersion in the life of the Triune God mediated in the canonical life of the church. This is how the church was birthed in the first place; this is how it has been sustained through the ages; and this is how it is renewed when it goes astray. There is no more pressing need than for the church to immerse itself in its own canonical traditions in a spirit of simple, decisive faith, and ready, continuous repentance.

SOME BACKGROUND ENCOURAGEMENT FROM PHILOSOPHERS

Two very important developments in the last twenty years should help in this process. First there is the remarkable turnaround in discussion about the intellectual viability of Christian belief. When I trained in philosophy in the late sixties, it was virtually impossible to find a really penetrating account of the rationality of religious belief. As a student I remember having to lie low as some of my instructors ridiculed Christianity. In private the best one could find was the writings of C. S. Lewis. Overall, philosophers saw the Christian faith as an ancient curiosity which had been discredited by the great drift of modern discussion. Most did not even take time to refute it; that task had already been done by Hume and Kant in an earlier generation, and, more recently, it had been splendidly executed by Logical Positiv-

ists like A. J. Ayer and Antony Flew, son of a very distinguished English Methodist theologian. In the face of three
hundred years of relentless criticism, many leading theologians had caved in, creating what we have called the third
schism in the body of the church.

Today the situation is radically different. In the last twenty
years there has been a remarkable reopening of the debate
about the rationality of the Christian faith. We are now in the
amazing position where there are extremely significant accounts of knowledge and credibility which make it entirely
feasible to provide a deep analysis of the truth of the Christian faith. The work of scholars like Basil Mitchell, Richard
Swinburne, Janet Martin Soskice, Alvin Plantinga, Nicholas
Wolterstorff, William Alston, Eleanor Stump, and a host of
others, has completely altered the landscape. Moreover,
there are small but significant signs that theologians are
beginning to take this work seriously.[7]

We must be very clear on the place of this kind of work in
the renewal of the church. As Gregory of Palamas pointed out
in the fourteenth century, we are not saved by philosophy.[8]
Philosophy is like hemlock. Prescribed by a doctor in the right
proportions and the correct circumstances, it can be invaluable; taken in the wrong doses it will kill the patient. Philosophy
can help in the intellectual recovery of nerve; it can make room
for faith in the face of constant social and intellectual criticism.
This is extremely important as we come to the end of the
modern age. It cannot, however, save our souls or renew the
church. For that we need the great acts of revelation and
redemption mediated to us in the canonical traditions of the
church through the working of the Holy Spirit.

A NEW NETWORKING IN ECUMENISM

The second remarkable development relevant to the recovery of the canonical traditions is the amazing ecumenical

relations which are currently in their initial formation. I have in mind here the fact that the old battle lines between Eastern and Western Christians, and, within the West, between classical Protestants and Roman Catholics are now thoroughly relativized. In the last ten years or so Evangelicals, Charismatics, and Pentecostals have begun to find their voices and to join in the discussion. I am not for one moment discounting the deep differences which exist between these traditions and which will continue to exist between these groups. On the contrary, I welcome the differences precisely because the debate within and between these traditions is exactly what is needed if we are to fathom the full riches of the tradition as a whole. The canonical traditions of the church both in terms of their identity and their content are essentially contested traditions. They are so rich and extended in their nature that different groups very naturally develop them in different directions. Hence we need all those who are committed to their continued existence to engage in a friendly struggle of interpretation and application which will bring out the best in them. The kind of deep, engaged ecumenical dialogue surfacing at present across the world between Roman Catholics, Pietists, Wesleyans, classical Anglicans, Lutherans and Calvinists, Pentecostals, the Eastern Orthodox, Charismatics, and even Fundamentalists, is exactly what is needed if we are to begin to grasp the extraordinary treasures given to us by the Holy Spirit in the history of the people of God. Even the contribution of those who have fought against the classical faith of the church can lend a hand, for a delicate balance of criticism and commitment will always be needed to prevent lethargy and complacency.

HOPE AHEAD FOR UNITED METHODISTS

Perceptive readers will by now have grasped the significance of our earlier argument on the identity of United

Methodist doctrine. Buried in the church are some of the materials crucially relevant to the renewal of the church as a whole. We do not have to reinvent the wheel. Our fore-fathers and foremothers were extraordinarily foresighted in their decisions to develop the profound doctrinal vision that they enshrined in the constitution. When Wesley and the early Methodists insisted that they had been guided by providence, they were entirely correct. They were led by the Holy Spirit to ensure that later generations would be equipped with those doctrinal materials which put their movement into touch with the great classical faith of the church across the ages. They were bold enough to add to that material those treasures which they themselves had received in their encounter with the gospel.

We can see now why it is so mistaken to take doctrine as an archaic legacy to be replaced at the first sign of trouble. The Christian faith is full of surprises, which can only be taken hold of as we proceed in faith to follow Christ in the church and serve him in the world. The medicine for the renewal of our minds only works if we take it in patience and humility. Much of what has been offered as a substitute has simply not worked. Hope lies in drinking deeply from the medicine that has been stored up for us in the bosom of the church.

THREE PRACTICAL SUGGESTIONS

If we are to receive these treasures then I would offer three practical suggestions which need to be implemented in our local churches. It is clearly not enough to lay out some grand diagnosis and prescription if the practical medicines are not furnished to heal the patient. Here are the three pills which we should consider taking, if we want to see substantial healing take effect.

First, in the area of evangelism, we need to find a way to reinvent the functional equivalent of the training process used extensively in the early church. At present evangelism has as its goal the proclamation of the gospel to as many people as possible, represented by television evangelism; or it is seen as simple conversion, as represented by many parachurch organizations; or it is construed as church growth, as represented by the central agencies of the mainline denominations. What is needed is a deep shift of direction in which evangelism focuses on initiation into the kingdom of God in the church.[9] Constitutive of this is the intentional grounding of Christian children and new believers in the faith as happened in the third-century and fourth-century church and as happened in the Methodist movement of the eighteenth century.[10]

Second, there are many in our churches who have had next to no formation in the faith. They have come in through cultural assimilation, or they have become members at a point where they received minimal help in getting hold of the faith for themselves. One of the best ways to further the process of serious initiation is to make use of the weekend retreat. In my own area the best means that I have seen of helping people own the faith for themselves is through the movement known either as "Cursillo" or as "The Walk to Emmaus." This is a seventy-two-hour retreat, which originated in the Roman Catholic church in Spain, and which is used extensively in the Southwest Texas Conference and elsewhere in our church throughout the world. The results have been quite dramatic over a period of ten years; thousands of people have found a way forward in their discipleship. I am well aware of the liabilities connected with this kind of movement, yet all strategies of renewal have a pathological dimension which I cannot explore here. However, I am prepared to say that, surveying the history of renewal over the last two centuries, I have seen nothing more effective in helping nominal Christians begin to find their feet in the faith. If it were supplemented by other kinds of efforts in initiation, the long-term results could be astonishing.

Third, the last and most obvious observation has to do with Christian education. We need a massive effort to deploy the time and resources available in Christian education to teaching the classical faith of the church in all its depth and breadth. The hardware is already in place for this, for we have lots of Sunday school classes and teachers. What we need is the software. We need to make a strong effort to find ways to teach the canonical traditions of the church comprehensively and creatively. Maybe a whole new set of ecumenical curriculum material could be developed. Maybe we could devise a way to provide help on a vast scale for teachers to introduce such material to our churches. Maybe we could persuade the Christian education profession to make such a project a top priority over a ten-year period. Whatever the means adopted, we need to find ways whereby church members can explore in depth the faith they were given in their baptism and confirmation.

A GOOD DOSE OF CAUTIOUS REALISM

I have offered in this chapter some preliminary comments on the concept of renewal, a relatively rich description of our present problems in the church, and a clear argument as to why United Methodists should be hopeful about the future. I would like to finish on a note of cautious realism.

I do not know what the future holds for the church. We may well be on the brink of new Dark Ages in our culture, where we will be fortunate if we are able to keep alive the faith for our grandchildren. We could also be on the brink of a whole new Awakening, a Third Great Awakening, which would be one more of those surprising works of God in the history of our culture. We should be discerning enough to be prepared for both possibilities. We should also, just to be on the safe side, be prepared for a time of soft discipleship and mediocre Christianity. Maybe what lies ahead is a journey into the wilderness. Whatever happens we know one thing: God in Christ has established the church by the power of the Holy Spirit, and the gates of hell will not prevail against it. Hence in the midst of our strivings, our worries, and our anxiety, we can always afford to take time to relax and hang loose. We are not in control of the renewal of Christ's church, and neither should we wish to be. For the power, the glory, the honor, and the final victory of faith and love are ultimately in the hands of the Father, and of the Son, and of the blessed and life-giving Holy Spirit. With this kind of assurance we can face any future in peace and confidence.

Within this assurance United Methodists can also tackle the thorny problem of the identity of their doctrinal standards. Pursuing this matter is not some sort of archaic exercise. The work of the last twenty years has not been in vain, for it has uncovered a vital treasure which lies waiting to be used. If I am right in what I have just suggested, the recovery of United Methodist doctrine is intimately related to the deep revitalization of the gospel in the church. It remains in a concluding chapter to spell out some more of the practical implications of my argument.

Chapter Five

What Then Shall We Do?

The argument to date has been simple. United Methodists really do have substantial, specific doctrinal commitments, which are enshrined in the very constitution of the church. The attempt to displace these and deploy the Methodist quadrilateral as an alternative to them is both unconstitutional and misguided. Moreover, the redeployment of this doctrine is critical to the welfare of the church in its worship, evangelism, and service to the world. Properly carried out, immersion in the historical faith of the church will work wonders in the deep healing and renewal of the church. It is time for the church as a whole and our leaders in particular to change our ways in the matter of doctrine and live up to our own internal identity.

What then are the practical implications of this analysis of our situation with respect to doctrine and doctrinal standards in The United Methodist Church? Let me try to answer this question by spelling out eight specific suggestions. I shall end with a brief epilogue.

A CLUTCH OF PRACTICAL SUGGESTIONS

1. Let me begin with a very mundane suggestion. Would it not be wise to restore the term "Doctrine" to the *Book of Discipline?* In other words, let us take appropriate action to

restore the title, "The Doctrines and Discipline," to the *Book of Discipline*. This would much better represent the changes made since 1968. Moreover it would send a clear signal that we really do think that doctrine is central to the way in which we organize and oversee the life of the church.

2. I suggest that it would also be wise for bishops to think through publicly with the church how they plan to own their responsibility for guarding the doctrinal tradition of the church. Within this we need to begin identifying some way or ways of holding them accountable in this area. At the moment this is uncharted territory, so we will clearly need time to work out how to proceed. Suffice it to say here that it was a good decision to put these matters in the hands of the bishops. The church needs an identifiable body to take responsibility for the supervision of doctrine, and the bishops are the natural agents to take this on board. Yet this must be done in such a way as to keep intact the responsibility of all the baptized for the propagation of the faith.

3. A strong effort needs to be mounted to introduce the laity at large to the doctrinal standards and the literature they have provoked. It is ludicrous to think that laity will seriously engage in the appropriation of doctrine or engage in theological reflection upon it and around it, if they are left in the dark and given no opportunity to encounter the material. There are hosts of educated and motivated laity who would be fascinated by United Methodist doctrine and theological reflection related thereto, if these were properly taught; they would also find their ministry and service deeply enhanced.

4. There is an urgent need for Boards of Ministry to face up to the changes that occurred at the General Conference of 1988. No doubt we need an extensive conversation on how to translate our commitment to the doctrinal standards of our church into appropriate forms of discernment and discipline in the examination of those who are candidates for

ordination. However, the time is long gone when we can rely on an outdated and constitutionally inappropriate appeal to the quadrilateral. We need to find ways to hold prospective ordinands accountable to the great classical doctrines of the faith, to the distinctives of our own tradition, and to the authority of scripture in matters of faith and practice. Here we will need lots of wisdom, but I suspect that it would not take too much effort to improve on the unfair and anarchic system which is currently in place. It is at this level that we can begin to take up the whole matter of how doctrinal supervision is to be exercised in a way that will be appropriate to a United Methodist ethos.

5. Far more attention needs to be given in seminary teaching to the doctrinal standards, to General Conference action and commentary thereon, and to the whole sweep of theological reflection in the Wesleyan tradition. At the moment work in these areas is far too marginal to be taken seriously. Extensive and rigorous study needs to be done of the standards themselves, in their historical and theological reception across the last two centuries, and in their vital relevance for the current scene. This is work which will require flair and imagination.

6. It would be a valuable exercise in self-examination to ask ourselves how we might revise our current liturgical traditions related to membership so that they might come to include the intellectual heritage of the church. This is a delicate and sensitive matter, as Wesley rightly recognized, for it is naturally the case that our growth in Christian knowledge is intimately related to our growth in grace. However, it is a counsel of despair to claim that we might not make progress here. We can surely find a creative way for new members to confess the apostolic faith of the church and the precious distinctives of our own tradition, as they join its members across the ages. Consider, for example, the possibility of adding the following questions. "Will you re-

ceive the treasures of the apostolic faith as enshrined in the doctrines of The United Methodist Church?" "Will you, with us, seek to order your life by those doctrines as the Holy Spirit works in you and in us to bring us to full spiritual maturity in Jesus Christ?" It is surely bizarre that our current materials do not even mention the name of Jesus Christ. I am well aware that the services of reception currently in the *United Methodist Hymnal* make ample provision for owning the classical faith of the church. However, in the circles in which I move this material is generally omitted, and a commitment to support the church by prayer, presence, gifts, and service is the standard usage. If the latter commitment continues to be used, then the improvements suggested here are surely in order.

7. It is surely fitting in the present context to appeal to all elders to ponder anew their responsibilities in the area of teaching the doctrines of The United Methodist Church. I think that this is inherent in their ordination vows, but that is a rather banal and juridical way to approach the issue. Elders of the church need to ponder and teach the great doctrines of the faith because they nourish the sheep under their care, because they heal us of our sins, and because they provide light and life for a lost world.

8. It would be equally fitting for the General Conference to appoint a standing Commission on Doctrine. I realize that the current mood in the country and the church is to resist the idea of adding one more committee to the life of our church. Moreover, given the alienation that exists in many quarters, it will not be easy to foster the kind of deep trust which will ultimately be needed, if the requisite work is to be done. However, such a move would continue the invaluable conversation which has developed over the last twenty years on doctrine. There is too much unfinished business and too many loose ends; and more business and loose ends are sure to appear on the horizon. We need a continuing

process which can act as an advisory clearinghouse for the church at large and for the Council of Bishops, and which can make appropriate material available from time to time.

Such a move would help the church as a whole engage in the continuing task of doctrinal and theological reflection. Our doctrines need to be related creatively to the life of the church and the world; there are new problems and insights to be pondered; and there are old issues to be revisited and extended. Hence, it is right to call the whole church to avoid intellectual laziness and indifference.

In this context we can take up the question of what to do with the current material in the *Book of Discipline* on the quadrilateral and related matters. We owe it to our great teachers to ponder these proposals about theological methodology. Their work constitutes contingent suggestions, endorsed by the General Conference during a period of great doctrinal confusion, which should be explored on merit and construed, for a time, as a kind of useful commentary. We need to do our very best to bind up the wounds of the mothers and fathers of the last generation. So long as we are clear about the content of our doctrines we can afford a measure of generosity in our construal of the epistemic sins of the last generation and make the best of their labors. More particularly this material highlights the need for extensive work in the theory of religious knowledge, that is, on matters pertaining to the question of canon and norm in Christian theology.

Such a commission should seriously consider other ways to enable United Methodists to engage in doctrinal and theological work rather than that currently made available in the *Discipline.* The attempt to develop theological guidelines for the tradition as a whole was initially too much of an effort to displace the actual doctrinal standards of the church for it to inspire confidence. Certainly this is how it has been interpreted, and the ensuing confusion has greatly damaged the status of the doctrinal heritage of the church. Moreover, it is unwise for the church as a whole to commit itself formally to a detailed theory of religious knowledge. In fact there are good arguments against the church's taking a stand on such matters. For instance, it is clear that these decisions are a matter of specialized philosophical competence, so the less said about them officially the better. Much can be left to the informal transmission of various proposals from one generation to another. However we resolve these claims, it is surely wise to take more time to study and ponder them than we have done to date. In this regard the work of a Commission on Doctrine could be extremely salutary, if it were properly orchestrated.

A FINAL WORD ON THE IMPORTANCE OF DOCTRINE

From the time I set out to develop the proposals I have argued for here, I have been acutely aware of the extent to which I am calling into question attitudes and positions which have long been taken for granted within United Methodism. Allow me to press again, however, the significance of doctrine for the church.

The crucial point to be made here is a simple one. In the end, the church cannot endure without a body of systematic and coherent doctrine. This was not the problem Wesley faced two centuries ago. His challenge was to take the doctrine the church already possessed in her canonical traditions and make it accessible to the masses of his day. Hence he did not make doctrine a high priority in his efforts to renew the church of his day. Two hundred years later, the situation is radically reversed. We have become so doctrinally indifferent and illiterate that the church is starved of intellectual content. Indeed, in many quarters the church has become internally secularized. It has no shared public discourse of its own, other than that borrowed from the secular world, to think through its pastoral care, its mission in the world, its evangelism, and its internal administration. Hence pastoral care is reduced to therapy, mission to sociopolitical action, evangelism to church growth, academic theology to amateur philosophical inquiry, and church administration to total quality management.

To be sure, only a fool would claim that we cannot learn from the best secular inquiries of our day, and only the indolent would fail to plunder the Egyptians of our own generation. Yet it is patently obvious that the Christian tradition has its own special way of thinking about its healing care, its mission, its evangelism, its internal structures, and the like. That special way of thinking is inescapably doctrinal. It takes us deep into discourse about God, creation, incarnation, salvation, and the host of materials which are deposited in the canonical traditions of the church. Moreover, one obvious purpose of doctrinal standards is to make available to every generation those doctrinal treasures which are the bedrock of Christian identity and renewal. Such treasures are especially pertinent for a generation, such as our own, that is liable to suffer from doctrinal dyslexia, if not doctrinal amnesia. The recovery of doctrinal identity is not then some abstract exercise in constitutional archaeology; it is integral to the deep renewal of the life and work of the church in the current generation.

Nor is this recovery a signal to throw down our theological tools and pretend there are no new issues to be taken up in our own day. On the contrary, it is the recovery of doctrine that in part makes one acutely aware how crucial continuing intellectual engagement is in the life of the church. We have to find our own way to deploy the doctrines of the faith and to offer the kind of interpretative investigation that will be relevant to our own times. We have to try to solve the problems and questions that lie buried in the tradition; we have to deal with a host of objections that occur to insiders and outsiders; and we have to make our own contributions to the life of the Christian mind. This continuing work is not done in a doctrinal vacuum. It is done precisely in and through the owning of the doctrines of the faith in our own space and time.

The burden of this book has rightly fallen on identifying what United Methodists must own as constitutive of their doctrines, as they meet the challenges of a new day and generation. The danger is not that United Methodists will cease to think. The danger is that they will believe that thinking United Methodists can think independently of those doctrines which are the lifeblood of their own historical faith and that of the Christian faith across the centuries.

Notes

CHAPTER ONE: UNITY AND DISUNITY IN THE UNITED METHODIST CHURCH

1. In 1988, several Protestant churches joined together in an "Ecumenical Decade: Churches in Solidarity with Women, 1988–1998." One of the programs sponsored in implementation of this Ecumenical Decade was a global theological colloquium of feminist and womanist theologians, entitled "Re-imagining," which took place November 4-7, 1993, in Minneapolis, Minnesota.

CHAPTER TWO: THE QUEST FOR DOCTRINAL STANDARDS

1. See Thomas Langford, *Practical Divinity: Theology in the Wesleyan Tradition* (Nashville: Abingdon Press, 1983).
2. See his "An Authentic Wesleyanism for Today," *Sinhak Gwa Saige, Theology and the World* 17 (1988): 97 (emphasis mine).
3. See Dietrich Bonhoeffer, *The Cost of Discipleship* (London: S.C.M. Press, 1959), p. 264 n. 1.
4. For an excellent discussion of the place of doctrine and theology in The United Methodist Church, see Thomas A. Langford, ed., *Doctrine and Theology in the United Methodist Church* (Nashville: Kingswood Books, 1991).
5. The most stimulating treatment of this is still Robert E. Chiles, *Theological Transition in American Methodism: 1790–1935* (Nashville/New York: Abingdon Press, 1965).
6. A very powerful and attractive expression of this can be found in the life of Borden Parker Bowne in the late nineteenth century.
7. Henceforth referred to simply as *Notes*.
8. There is a deep ambivalence in the thinking behind this move. If the content of the doctrinal standards is fundamentally a matter of historical interest, then this kind of concern to separate core from distinctives is really of secondary importance. However, this distinction proves to be crucial in later interpretations of the doctrinal content of the tradition.

Notes

9. I use the term "Methodist quadrilateral" rather than "Wesleyan quadrilateral" in order at this point to avoid disputes about how far the quadrilateral can be traced to the work of John Wesley.

10. It is often thought that the appeal to scripture, tradition, reason, and experience is a uniquely Methodist move. This is far from the case, for one finds it also among modern Anglicans, like James A. Pike, W. Norman Pittenger, and Randolph Crump Miller. See Robert W. Prichard, "The Place of Doctrine in the Episcopal Church," in Ephraim Radner and George R. Sumner, eds., *Reclaiming Faith, Essays on Orthodoxy in the Episcopal Church and the Baltimore Declaration* (Grand Rapids: Wm. B. Eerdmans, 1993), pp. 38-39. I am also well aware that United Methodists are tempted to argue that everybody, whether they acknowledge it or not, is committed to these norms. It is perhaps best to treat this as an excusable example of absentminded triumphalism.

11. *Book of Discipline* (1984), p. 78. Note how in this proposal the boundaries originally construed in terms of particular doctrines are intentionally replaced by boundaries construed in terms of theological method.

12. This is the language used in the First Restrictive Rule of the Constitution. See the *Book of Discipline*, p. 25.

13. Richard Heitzenrater, "At Full Liberty: Doctrinal Standards in Early American Methodism," in *Mirror and Memory, Reflections on Early American Methodism* (Nashville: Kingswood Books, 1989), pp. 189-204.

14. See Thomas C. Oden, *Doctrinal Standards in the Wesleyan Tradition* (Grand Rapids: Francis Asbury Press, 1988).

15. Heitzenrater nicely captures the crucial distinction at issue by speaking of the *Articles* and *Confession* as being a matter of law, while the *Sermons* and *Notes* represent the weight of tradition.

16. I am very grateful to the reverend Dr. James Mayfield for bringing this to my attention.

17. *Book of Discipline* (1988), p. 81.

18. *Book of Discipline* (1988), p. 86.

19. *Book of Discipline* (1988), pp. 77-78.

20. By far the most penetrating discussion of pluralism has been provided by Jerry L. Walls in *The Problem of Pluralism* (Wilmore, Ky.: Bristol Books, 1988). Walls makes a compelling case that this is an incoherent notion. His work has not received the attention his arguments merit.

CHAPTER THREE: THE SEARCH FOR DOCTRINAL IDENTITY

1. *The Problem of Pluralism* (Wilmore, Ky.: Bristol Books, 1988).

2. It does not make it absolutely impossible. This was the situation the church had to face when the merger took place in 1968. At that time the addition of the *Confession of Faith* to the *Articles of Religion* was deemed not to be contrary to the designated standards.

3. For an important essay on this topic see Ted A. Campbell, "The 'Wesleyan Quadrilateral': The Story of a Modern Methodist Myth," in Thomas A. Langford, ed., *Doctrine and Theology in the United Methodist Church* (Nashville: Kingswood Books, 1991), pp. 154-61. See also the forthcoming book by Scott Jones, *John Wesley's Conception and Use of Scripture* (Nashville, 1995), on Wesley's position more generally on authority. This is to be published by Kingswood Books; it is likely to become the standard work on this topic.

4. I am grateful to Charles Merrell for helping me to phrase this point in this way.

5. Most of the canons of the church, such as the Holy Scriptures and the early creeds, are deeply misunderstood when they are treated as some kind of epistemic norm. The shift from canon to norm in all likelihood took place in the wake of the Reformation disputes about the relative merits of scripture and tradition in the church.

6. I leave aside entirely at this point the fact that it is not at all clear what good it would do to invoke the quadrilateral as a doctrinal standard. The very terms *scripture, tradition, reason,* and *experience* can be interpreted in such radically diverse ways, that to appeal to the quadrilateral is functionally the equivalent of appealing to a norm that is empty of content. Its friends seem to think that this is a virtue, not realizing that they are engaged in an exercise of self-destruction. See, for example, Thomas A. Langford, "The United Methodist Quadrilateral: A Theological Task," in Langford, ed., *Doctrine and Theology*, pp. 232-44.

7. This claim has to be tempered by the fact that the liturgies for baptism, confirmation, and reaffirmation of faith, reception into The United Methodist Church, and reception into the local congregation, all make use of the Apostles' Creed. Interestingly, no variation is allowed here. See the *United Methodist Hymnal,* pp. 33-54.

CHAPTER FOUR: DOCTRINAL HEALING AND THE RENEWAL OF THE CHURCH

1. William G. McLoughlin, *Revivals, Awakenings, and Reform* (Chicago: University of Chicago Press, 1978).

2. See *The Great Awakening* (New Haven: Yale University Press, 1972), pp. 353-58. Before we dismiss Edwards as a rational chauvinist, it is worth remembering that Christians of all nations tend to believe in the favored status of their own nation. I am grateful to Yam Kai Lee for drawing this to my attention.

3. Dean M. Kelly's *Why Conservative Churches Are Growing* (New York: Harper & Row, 1972) was a crucial text in the opening of the debate.

4. Readers may pursue these varied proposals in the following books: John Leith, *From Generation to Generation* (Louisville: Westminster/John Knox Press, 1990); Rosemary Ruether, "The Free Church Movement in Contemporary Catholicism," in Martin E. Marty and Dean G. Peerman, *New Theology No 6* (New York: Macmillan, 1969), and *Sexism and God-talk* (Boston: Beacon Press, 1983); Lesslie

Notes

Newbigin, *The Other Side of 1984* (Geneva: WCC, 1984); James Draper, *Authority: The Crucial Issue for Southern Baptists* (Old Tappan, N.J.: Revell, 1984); Leon Cardinal Suenens, *A New Pentecost?* (New York: Seabury, 1975); Alexander Schmemann, *Eucharist: Sacrament of the Kingdom* (Crestwood, N.Y.: St. Vladimir's Seminary Press, 1991); Thomas Oden, *Agenda for Theology* (San Francisco: Harper & Row, 1979); John Milbank, *Theology and Social Theory, Beyond Secular Reason* (Oxford: Blackwell, 1992); Basil Mitchell, *Morality: Religious and Secular* (Oxford: Clarendon, 1980); Alasdair MacIntyre, *After Virtue* (Notre Dame: University of Notre Dame Press, 1981); Charles Taylor, *Sources of the Self* (Cambridge: Harvard University Press, 1989).

5. Precisely what modernity is and how it began is, of course, a matter for widespread discussion. For example, see Louis Dupré, *Passage to Modernity* (New Haven: Yale University, 1993).

6. I owe this comment to personal conversation with Dr. Andrew Walker of the University of London.

7. I briefly discuss these developments in "The State of Christian Theology in North America," in Mortimer J. Adler, ed., *The Great Ideas Today* (Chicago: Encyclopedia Britannica, 1991), pp. 242-86.

8. Gregory Palamas, *The Triads* (New York: Paulist, 1983), pp. 25-29.

9. I have argued this case at length in *The Logic of Evangelism* (Grand Rapids: Wm. B. Eerdmans, 1989).

10. I have sought to pursue this possibility by developing, in liaison with First United Methodist Church, Uvalde, Texas, a fourteen-week course called *Basic Christianity*, which will shortly be made available through The United Methodist Publishing House.

Index

Index

Index

Index